Marriage Made in HEAVEN

McDougal & Associates
Servants of Christ and Stewards of the Mysteries of God

Marriage Made in HEAVEN

by

Desmond Thomas

Unless otherwise noted, all scripture quotations are from the Authorized King James Version of the Bible, public domain. All scripture word definitions are from *Strong's Exhaustive Concordance* of the Bible, Dugan Publishers, Inc., Gordonsville, Tennessee.

Marriage Made in Heaven
Copyright © 2017 — by Desmond A. S. Thomas
All rights reserved under U.S. and international copyright conventions. Contents and/or cover may not be reproduced in whole or in part in any form without the express written consent of the publisher. No part of this book may be reproduced or transmitted in any form or by any means, electronic or mechanical, including photocopying, recording or by any information retrieval system.

Disclaimer: These teachings are drawn from the Holy Scriptures and backed up by the experience of many wise practitioners. However, what you will read in this book is not intended as the only diagnosis of problems you may have in your life. Help and counseling advice may be sought from others, and the writer in no way seeks to turn you away from the role they have to play in meeting your particular marital needs.

Cover Design by Paulo Sergio Silva

Published by:

McDougal & Associates
18896 Greenwell Springs Road
Greenwell Springs, LA 70739
www.thepublishedword.com

McDougal & Associates is dedicated to the spreading of the Gospel of Jesus Christ to as many people as possible in the shortest time possible.

ISBN 978-0-9543083-7-7

Printed in the US, the UK and Australia
For Worldwide Distribution

Dedication

This book is dedicated to all who believe in the institution of Christian marriage.

To all those who are entering into the marriage covenant for the very first time.

To those who are struggling to make their marriage work and to keep it going in love and in faith.

To all who refuse to give up on their marriage.

To those who have failed in marriage before. I trust that, by reading this book and applying its principles, you will make it this time.

Acknowledgements

I have long wanted to write a book about marriage. Looking back, I guess I may not have acquired sufficient knowledge and experience on this subject until now. I thank God for giving me the knowledge and experience I now have and the opportunity to write this book at this appointed time. Thank You, Heavenly Father.

I thank my wife Mary for being my faithful wife all these years and for giving me three beautiful sons. I could not have asked for anything more from a wife, mother of my sons and companion in ministry. Thank you, Mary.

I thank my boys, Steven, Melchizedek and Desmond, Jr., for the experience of being a father to them and for their love and support for our ministry. Also for being a part of our music department in the church, I thank you. Thank you, sons.

Dr. Harold and Andy McDougal, words cannot express my appreciation of your love for me and Mary, that in the midst of your greatest financial need you can still sow a seed into our ministry by giving us the opportunity to publish this book. You have sowed into my life from my teenage years, as teacher and mentor, and now you are publishing my words to the world. Thank you, publisher and mentor.

To Paulo and Vania, you are an inspiration to me. Thank you for your love and example, and thank you for your friendship. Thank you for desiring my success and prosperity in ministry. I also thank you for your purity of heart. Thank you, my friend.

Thanks to all who will buy and read this book. May its content be a blessing to you, as you strive to have a *Marriage Made in Heaven*. Thank you all, in Jesus' name. Amen!

Contents

Foreword by Raymond de' Souza George ... .11
Introduction 13
Author's Preface 16

1. Definitions 19
2. Understanding the Marriage Covenant.................27
3. Understanding the Institution of Marriage 33
4. Understanding the Importance of Agreement...........55
5. Understanding the Need for Compatibility 77
6. Understand What Love Is... 93
7. Understanding Your Roles, Functions and Responsibilities...103
8. Understanding How to Properly Divide Your Time .119
9. Understanding Blessings that Can Destroy 127
10. Understanding the Importance of Good Communication 135
11. Understanding the Promise: "Till Death Do Us Part"..141
    The Conclusion..147

Other Books by Desmond Thomas..........................149
Author Contact Page..154

LOVE NEVER FAILS

1 Corinthians 13:8, ASV

Foreword by Raymond de' Souza George

If I was allowed only two words, I would say, of *Marriage Made In Heaven*, ESSENTIAL and ACCESSIBLE. Marriage is a journey that must be willingly undertaken in a serious frame of mind, by a man and a woman humble enough to seek clearance from the Divine Architect of that institution. The climate that will challenge their relationship throughout the journey is fully known only to Him, the Designer. In order, therefore, to successfully negotiate the challenges, every participant (or intending participant) must acknowledge the necessity for His continuous oversight, with their fullest cooperation.

Marriage Made In Heaven has just made me realize, that even after forty years of wedlock, there's SO MUCH MORE still to learn about God's first institution, and the expectations of those who enter. In the face of the current universal perversion of this institution, it is necessary for the world to be reminded of God's intention for those who fancy His design.

What a product! Brother Desmond's unique combination of humility, devotion, diligence and sincerity fully qualify him to minister to his stipulated audience.

Christian marriage is under threat universally, and *Marriage Made In Heaven*, by its structure, is an appropriate prescription.

The content page is uniquely flavored with the word *understanding*. This points to a lack which has helped the devil to attack marriages, homes and families. In my view, therefore, this work accurately diagnoses and prescribes in a very simple and accessible way, the needs and how to meet them.

To all those seeking a redefinition of God's design for human co-existence and multiplication, this is a God-pleasing gift. In addition, it meets the needs of marriages in all states, people in courtship and even divorced couples.

Let me highlight two points raised in the tenth chapter dealing with "Understanding the Importance of Good Communication."

- "Never forget to say, 'I'm sorry' when you have messed up."
- "Never stop saying, 'I love you.'"

If you are too big or too good to say "I'm sorry," you may not be trusted when you say "I love you." These are the drops of water and grains of sand which make the mighty oceans and beauteous land of marriage.

> *If any of you lack wisdom, let him ask of God, that giveth to all men liberally and upbraideth not; and it shall be given him.* James 1:5

This is what *Marriage Made In Heaven* can do for us. Make it a must-read in your home.

Raymond de' Souza George

Introduction

Life is busy, life is getting busier, and I think life is at its busiest since Creation. Life is so busy that physical relationships are becoming ever more distant. We are living in an electronic world. Work is done electronically, shopping is done electronically, banking is done electronically, the postal service is accessed electronically, social meetings are now conducted as social networks, and even many relationships are now little more than virtual relationships. I even understand there is a thing called "speed dating" being used these days because people don't have time to meet and get to know each other in the normal way.

One would think that the speed at which things can be done would have provided more time for recreation and the development of personal relationships, but unfortunately that is not the case. Other things have robbed us of family time, things like the pursuit of a career, the use of modern technology, and the pursuit of wealth. These have all eaten into the fabric of family life.

Aside from this business of life, people today are trying to redefine everything else. The gay and lesbian world wants marriage redefined, and pressure is now being put on the Church to change its stance in this regard. The liberal world is even questioning the very significance of marriage in this twenty-first century.

The increase of sin and the decay of morality have also threatened marital relationships, breaking the marriage and family structure. Regard for the sanctity of marriage is at an all-time low, and divorce continues its rampage, even among Christians. So what is the future of this first God-given institution?

The purpose of this book is to reestablish in our minds and spirits God's full intention and His perfect will for marriages, our marriages. It is to encourage us to hold on to the biblical values regarding this all important institution. For some, I believe this book can throw new light on the subjects of what the marriage relationship is all about, bringing us back to God's perspective, so that His will for our marriages can be established in us.

I pray that this book will help us build strong relationships, understand our various roles in the family, and put our priorities in order. I pray that it will help us to recognize the things that threaten the twenty-first century Christian family and enable us to fight against them. Marriage is that which illustrates in a practical way our relationship with Jesus Christ, our Lord and Savior, and we don't want to lose that experience.

Can our Christian marriages survive the things that threaten its survival? Of cause it can. The answers are found in God's Word. The One who instituted marriage in the first place has all the answers we need for it. So let's see what God has to say on this subject, and then we can take practical steps, not only to save our rela-

INTRODUCTION

tionships, but also to enjoy them. If we do that , phrases like, "we grew apart," and "we fell out of love" will be phrases of the past. As we study this subject together, please remember this most important point:

If we can learn about God's desire for marriage, we can have a *Marriage Made in Heaven.*

Desmond Thomas
London, England

Author's Preface

It is my opinion that individualism is the greatest threat to our society today. The concept of "I", "Me" and "Myself" is ruining every strata of society. What-is-in-it-for-me?" and other similar thought processes like it have destroyed society as a whole, and marriage has suffered as a result. The more wealthier the world becomes, the more families grow apart.

Political parties, businesses, church groups and musical groups that should have become stronger and gone global are still mediocre because they operate as individuals and not as a team. Sport teams would have won championships over and over again, if they had been a team, but because one person has to shine above the rest, they continue to lose. The god of this world is breaking apart society bit by bit, and our marriages and homes have become victims to his disease.

Promoters, managers, and lawyers all contribute to individualism. They will tell you how it is *your* name and your name alone that should be up in neon lights. They will tell you that the others around you are a crowd and that they are taking up *your* space. One lawyer asked a woman, her client, "Do you know how much your husband is worth? And do you know what *your* share of that wealth will be if you divorce him?" Today it is how much

AUTHOR'S PREFACE

can you can get from another person, a company or an insurance agency for an accident you suffered. Someone must pay, and each of us seems dedicated to getting as much a we can get, anyway we can get it. This is the society in which we live.

Our Lord Jesus Christ, by word and by example, taught us sacrifice, but sacrifice for the general good of others is no longer regarded as correct comportment. It is dog eat dog, and may the best man win.

The breakdown of marriage in the twenty-first century, even among Christians, can be traced directly to this individualism:

I'm not happy in this marriage.
What about my needs?
I'm not here to solve his [or her] problems; let him [or her] sort them out. I have nothing to do with that.
I need to concentrate on what makes me happy.

This is not what our Lord has taught us. He said:

Brethren, if a man be overtaken in a fault, ye which are spiritual, restore such an one in the spirit of meekness; considering thyself, lest thou also be tempted. Bear ye one another's burdens, and so fulfill the law of Christ. For if a man think himself to be something, when he is nothing, he deceiveth himself.   Galatians 6:1-3

In marriage, two become one, and everything in our marriage ceremony points to that fact. Vows are taken, committing the two of us to becoming one. One ring is given by each party to the other. One cake is consumed, indicating the one flesh that is the result of a man and a woman joining in holy matrimony. There can be no individualism in marriage, and if there is, it must be an individual of two. Everything about marriage must be the opposite of the individualism the world teaches so ardently today. If we can just rededicate ourselves to the will of God concerning marriage, we will be richly rewarded with the joys He intended marriage to bring us. He wants us to have a *Marriage Made in Heaven.*

CHAPTER 1

Definitions

To understand God's design for marriage, we need to first understand the creation of man and of woman, their order of creation, and their functions, as they were originally prescribed by God. The origin and purpose of anything gives us a perfect understanding of its function, and this is no more true than with marriage. Marriage is God's idea, and God designed it, so we need to understand His original intent for it.

Understanding marriage must begin with the definition of the words *man* and *woman*. In the first marriage, there was a man and a woman who entered into union. Therefore, by understanding the meaning and function of these words, we can understand the meaning of marriage.

WHAT IS MAN?

Man was created in the image and likeness of God and is the most versatile of God's creations. Man is one specie. There are various species of birds, cats, and dogs, but man is a single and unique specie. *Man* is a short form of the word *mankind*. Whether a man is a Negro, Caucasian, Asian, Hispanic or Eskimo, he is a man and part of mankind.

Every species has both male and female. In man's species, the male is called *man,* and the female is called *woman.* When God is talking, in general terms, about *man* in the Scriptures, He is talking about mankind, both male and female. For instance:

> *And God said, Let us make man in our image, after our likeness: and let them have dominion over the fish of the sea, and over the fowl of the air, and over the cattle, and over all the earth, and over every creeping thing that creepeth upon the earth. So God created man in his own image, in the image of God created he him; male and female created he them. And God blessed them, and God said unto them, Be fruitful, and multiply, and replenish the earth, and subdue it: and have dominion over the fish of the sea, and over the fowl of the air, and over every living thing that moveth upon the earth.*   Genesis 1:26-28

In Creation, God referred to Himself as *Us* and *Our.* Then He created man in His own image and after His own likeness. Here we see the plurality of God (Elohim), and we also see the plurality of man. God, referring to man, called him *them, male and female.* So we see that man is both male and female. The two elements combined makes the complete man. God created them male and female, making man one completed being.

This perfect male and female then received the blessing of fruitfulness and increase, which represented the procreation and continuation of the human race. In fact, all of God's living creatures received that pronouncement of blessing. He had made all of these creatures male and female.

DEFINITIONS

THE MAN REPRESENTS GOD

The man was created first, so he is the head. He was created before the woman and was made in the image and likeness of God, so he comes first as head of the marital union.

The man was made leader of his home. This does not have anything to do with his intelligence or natural abilities; it is just how God designed things to be. Man was given leadership by order of creation and by the role he was given to perform. So being a man means being first and it means being the head of the woman.

This also means that man functions as Christ's representative in the home. He is the priest and lord of his household:

> *But I suffer not a woman to teach, nor to usurp authority over the man, but to be in silence. For Adam was first formed, then Eve. And Adam was not deceived, but the woman being deceived was in the transgression. Notwithstanding she shall be saved in childbearing, if they continue in faith and charity and holiness with sobriety.*
> 1 Timothy 2:12-15

So we see that the authority in the home is the man, and the woman should not usurp that authority. Adam was not the one who was deceived, but the woman, and by virtue of that deception, she was also made to be subject to the man. We can now conclude that man means: representative of Christ, head, priest and authority in the home.

Unto the woman he said, I will greatly multiply thy sorrow and thy conception; in sorrow thou shalt bring forth children; and thy desire shall be to thy husband, and he shall rule over thee. Genesis 3:16

WHAT IS WOMAN?

And the Lord *God said, It is not good that the man should be alone; I will make him an help meet for him.*
And the Lord *God caused a deep sleep to fall upon Adam, and he slept: and he took one of his ribs, and closed up the flesh instead thereof; and the rib, which the* Lord *God had taken from man, made he a woman, and brought her unto the man. And Adam said, This is now bone of my bones, and flesh of my flesh: she shall be called Woman, because she was taken out of Man.* Genesis 2:18 and 21-23

We next see that a rib was taken from the side of the man to form a woman. The word *women* means, *"taken out of man."* The woman came second and was made as a companion to the man. God made the woman for the man. The woman was made in the image of the man, from a rib from His side. Woman then means: "second, companion and helper of the man."

After the birth of their first sons, Adam called his wife Eve (mother), because she was the *"mother of all living"* (Genesis 3:20).

WHO WAS EVE?

Eve was the mother of all living. This is what Adam called his wife. The other role of the woman is that of

DEFINITIONS

mother. Even though the woman was created for the man and the woman was taken out of the man, God has designed that the woman would then become the mother of all living. The mother will be the incubator and nurturer for the continuity of the human race, even though God is the Creator of all things.

WOMAN, AS THE GLORY OF MAN

> *For a man indeed ought not to cover his head, forasmuch as he is the image and glory of God: but the woman is the glory of the man.*
> *Nevertheless neither is the man without the woman, neither the woman without the man, in the Lord. For as the woman is of the man, even so is the man also by the woman; but all things of God.*
> 1 Corinthians 11:7 and 11-12

The woman is the glory of the man. This word *glory* means "dignity, honor, praise and worship." That is what the woman is to the man. I believe these are things a woman must get from her husband. If a man does not honor and have respect for his partner, if he treats her like dirt and tells her she is no good for anything, if he does not dignify and praise her, I don't believe he is a suitable candidate for marriage. The woman should be the glory of the man, and that dignity must originate with him.

> *But if a woman have long hair, it is a glory to her: for her hair is given her for a covering.*   1 Corinthians 11:15

The Bible says that the woman's hair is her glory. Women love to fix their hair in lovely ways for any special occasion, and when they spend so much time having their hair just right, they like to be complimented. The man must glorify her. If a man does not realize this, it is the duty of the woman to teach him. Ladies, if your partner does not praise you, introduce you to his friends or honor you in public and never seems to want to go out in public places with you, I think you should reconsider marrying him. You should be his glory or the marriage won't work.

IN SUMMARY

We can now draw a conclusion from this chapter. God made the marriage union, comprised of a male and a female, in complete harmony making one flesh. In this union, he made the man first (in His image and likeness) to be the head of the union. He then made the woman second (in the glory of the man) as a companion and helper to the man and a mother for the continuity of their species.

> *And the* Lord *God said, It is not good that the man should be alone; I will make him an help meet for him.*
> Genesis 2:18

The woman in this relationship must be a suitable helper. When considering the choice of a proper life's partner, a man needs to ask himself the question: How suitable is this woman for me? How can she complete me? What is lacking in me that she can add? Mature men look for completion in a woman, but macho men think they are

DEFINITIONS

sufficient in themselves and are threatened by the strength of a partner.

The woman also must see what help she can bring to a man's life. Ladies, if you feel there is no way you can be of help to him, then you'd better find someone you can complete. This is not your man.

Seeing a flaw in a man or a woman can be a positive thing—if you can see yourself helping to fix it. The first problem many have in finding a suitable husband or wife is that they are looking for a perfect person, and they do not exist. The key, rather, is for both man and woman to be able to look for completion in each other.

It is not good for a man to be alone. God said it. Research shows that most of the men who get into trouble are single. If they had a woman in their lives, their troubles might be prevented. God intended for you to have a *Marriage Made in Heaven*.

Chapter 2

Understanding the Marriage Covenant

"Why marry," one may ask? Well, I guess for someone with no faith, cohabiting without the benefit of marriage is the right thing. Others might ask, "If I love someone, why do I have to make a lasting vow to them?" Well, the purpose of this book is not to answer all the questions of "why" but explaining "what" marriage is. Marriage is a covenant ordained by God between a man and a woman, and that covenant is that they will spend the rest of their lives together. Jesus said:

> *Wherefore they are no more twain, but one flesh. What therefore God hath joined together, let not man put asunder.* Matthew 19:6

God instituted the covenant relationship of marriage so that men could avoid the loneliness Adam experienced in the Garden of Eden. God Himself decided that it was not good for a man to be alone. Therefore God instituted the marriage relationship between a man and a woman for their fellowship and intimacy.

God gave the man a job to do so that he could provide for himself, but then He said, "I will find a suitable helpmeet for him." No man is an island, so God gave the man a support system (and it works both ways).

Sex was then given to the man and the woman within this marriage system for their pleasure and intimacy and for the procreation and the continuity of the human race:

> *And the LORD God said, It is not good that the man should be alone; I will make him an help meet for him.*
> Genesis 2:18

> *Therefore shall a man leave his father and his mother, and shall cleave unto his wife: and they shall be one flesh.*
> Genesis 2:24

Some may still argue that they can do without getting married, but God said that sex and procreation should be reserved for the marriage. Sex is what seals the marriage covenant, and without the covenant there is nothing to seal.

GOD'S PART IN MARRIAGE

Since marriage is a covenant ordained by God, God must be called to the ceremony to join the couple. He must be called upon to put His seal on their covenant. In short, prayers must be said, prayers that seal this man and his bride together in a spiritual way, and where both God and man stand as witnesses.

THE NECESSARY VOWS

The man and his bride then make a covenant before God and the other witnesses to share with each other their bodies and all their earthly goods, as long as they shall live.

For the Christian, this is all done in the name of Jesus, and that seals the covenant. Anything we ask the Father in the name of Jesus, He will do it.

The vows then end with a declaration and pronouncement that this man and this woman are now husband and wife, and what God has joined together man must not separate. The man then unveils the bride and gives her a kiss, after the announcement: "You may now kiss the bride."

THE EXCHANGE OF RINGS

At some point in the majority of Christian wedding ceremonies, the man and the woman exchange the gift of rings. These rings symbolize an unending union. Whenever they see those rings in the future, they will be reminded of their covenant with one another. The ring then becomes a token or sign that the person wearing it is in a covenant relationship with another.

THE PRONOUNCEMENTS OF BLESSING

At the end of most weddings, blessings are pronounced on the man and the woman, who are now one because of the marriage covenant they have sworn to uphold. These are blessings of fruitfulness, procreation, health and prosperity.

THE SIGNING OF DOCUMENTS

After the formalities of a Christian wedding, the man

and his wife then sign legal papers that serve as proof of their agreement in marriage and legalize their union.

THE COVENANT MEAL

Most couples then attend a reception, where they greet their well-wishers, eat together a covenant mean, and cut and partake of the covenant cake. This reception often includes the first marriage dance.

THE FINAL CONSUMMATION

It is, of course, the sexual union of the man and woman that completes their marriage, and most couples embark on some form of honeymoon. When alone, the husband and the wife now meet in sexual union, thereby consummating their marriage. Blood is mingled, making both bodies one flesh—literally.

A PERFECT COVENANT

Those who have studied covenants would surely agree with me that the marriage covenant is a perfect example. All biblical covenants had many things in common:

1. God was always mentioned or called to witness the covenant:

Yet ye say, Wherefore? Because the LORD hath been witness between thee and the wife of thy youth, against whom thou hast dealt treacherously: yet is she thy companion, and the wife of thy covenant.   Malachi 2:14

2. Blessings were pronounced upon those who were obedient to the covenant, and sometimes curses

were pronounced upon those who were disobedient to the covenant:

And all these blessings shall come on thee, and overtake thee, if thou shalt hearken unto the voice of the LORD thy God. Deuteronomy 28:2

3. On many occasions a blood sacrifice was made as a seal to the covenant or, as with Abraham, the covenant was sealed in the circumcision of his flesh:

This is my covenant, which ye shall keep, between me and you and thy seed after thee; Every man child among you shall be circumcised. And ye shall circumcise the flesh of your foreskin; and it shall be a token of the covenant betwixt me and you.
Genesis 17:10-11

4. Lastly, a covenant meal or feast was made to commemorate and celebrate the covenant:

And this day shall be unto you for a memorial; and ye shall keep it a feast to the LORD throughout your generations; ye shall keep it a feast by an ordinance for ever.
Exodus 12:14

The covenant of marriage is a very solemn one and we are warned that when we make a promise, we must keep that promise:

UNDERSTANDING THE MARRIAGE COVENANT

When thou vowest a vow unto God, defer not to pay it; for he hath no pleasure in fools: pay that which thou hast vowed. Better is it that thou shouldest not vow, than that thou shouldest vow and not pay.   Ecclesiastes 5:4-5

The marriage vows are part of the marriage covenant, and they are meant to be kept. When a man and a woman are joined in marriage, they agree to share their debts and also their possessions and any future prosperity. What is hers becomes his, and what is his becomes hers. The same is true of his and her body. The Scriptures put it this way:

Let the husband render unto the wife due benevolence: and likewise also the wife unto the husband. The wife hath not power of her own body, but the husband: and likewise also the husband hath not power of his own body, but the wife. Defraud ye not one the other, except it be with consent for a time, that ye may give yourselves to fasting and prayer; and come together again, that Satan tempt you not for your incontinency.   1 Corinthians 7:3-5

Since the man is the head of the house, the woman then traditionally takes his name, and they become one family. From this point on, they will have a common ancestry.

It is our practice that both the man and the woman go through deliverance ministration, if they have not done so before, because any generational curse or negative ancestry covenant in both families that has not be broken can be inherited in this newly-formed family.

MARRIAGE MADE IN HEAVEN

Marriage is a covenant of sharing. You commit yourself to it by making a vow before God and man. You symbolize it through gifts and a covenant meal. You receive the blessings of God Almighty to keep it. If you have not entered marriage yet, keep this in mind before you enter it. If you are already married, understand the covenant you have entered into. May God bless you, and may you have a happy marriage in Jesus name.

Amen!

Indeed, may you have a *Marriage Made in Heaven!*

CHAPTER 3

Understanding the Institution of Marriage

WHAT IS MARRIAGE?

All sorts of flowery words and phrases have been used to define marriage. Someone said that it is "an institution wherein the man loses his Bachelors and the woman gains her Masters." Some believers look at marriage only as a license for having sex, whereas others come into it for the social status they hope to gain. Marriage, for others, is a means for obtaining financial security or a respectable status. Many people come into this God-given institution with their own ideas or reasons, which are often quite different from what the other party may be considering. Having opposing views about marriage makes it difficult for the marriage to work. Two cannot work together unless they agree. Our varied ideas, traditions and cultural backgrounds make for marriage conflicts. Therefore both parties need to come to a common understanding of the concept of marriage.

In a Christian marriage, the Bible supersedes all culture and tradition. The Bible forms the foundation for

Christian marriage, and both parties must commit themselves to conform to its standards. In order for a marriage to be successful, the two parties must dedicate themselves to studying the Word of God on this subject and undergoing counseling from experienced spiritual leaders and other authorities on the subject. Even those with a wealth of experience on this subject must put their concepts under the microscope of the Word of God for examination and adjust them accordingly.

Although Mary and I were both pastors before we got married, we submitted ourselves to three other pastors for premarital counseling. We listened carefully to what they had to say and asked them questions on several matters. Then, together we decided on what we wanted for our marriage, in the light of the Scriptures.

Marriage is an honorable institution ordained by God. A man leaves his mother and father and is joined to his wife, thereby becoming one flesh. The two form an independent family, separate from the families they came from. The husband then becomes the head of that new home, and his wife becomes his helper. In this union, the man also becomes the priest and breadwinner of the home, and the woman becomes the homemaker.

In marriage, the man and woman forsake all others and cling to each other, becoming one flesh. And God warns that what He has put together, none should separate. This is the way we honor the very first institution God initiated on earth.

A married couple needs to know the order God has designed for their marriage. In this order, God is the Head of their union, the man is the head of his wife, the wife is next to her husband, and then come the children of this union (see Hebrews 13:4, Genesis 2:24, Matthew 19:4-6, 1 Corinthians 6:16 and 11:3).

LEAVING, CLEAVING AND BECOMING ONE FLESH

These words *leave, cleave* and *one flesh* are used at least three times in the Scriptures. God used it during the creation of Eve and the instituting of the first marriage (see Genesis 2). Jesus used it when He was teaching about divorce (see Matthew 19). The the apostle Paul used it at least twice, once when he was teaching against committing fornication (see 1 Corinthians 6), and the other when he was teaching about Christian marriage (see Ephesians 5). So we can conclude that leaving, cleaving and becoming one flesh:

1. Defines and describes the union of marriage
2. Warns against sinning against the union through divorce, and
3. Warns against dishonoring the marriage through extra-marital sex

Therefore shall a man leave his father and his mother, and shall cleave unto his wife: and they shall be one flesh. And they were both naked, the man and his wife, and were not ashamed. Genesis 2:24-25

THE LEAVING

Strong's describes the word *leaving* as being from the root word meaning "to relinquish, forsake and be destitute" (H5800) of mother and father. These are strong words, but they show us that God is asking the man and his wife both to relinquish themselves of their mothers and fathers and, in fact, considering themselves destitute of mother and father.

In marriage, a man leaves his parents home, joins himself to his own wife through marriage, and starts his own family. This means that neither the man nor his wife are now under the control of their parents or the rules of their house. They have left the dominion of their parent's home and started their own family, so now they are the heads of their own household. Their parents were the head of the house where they once lived, but now their parents have no jurisdiction over them or their new home. It is their home, and they are the masters of it.

This *leaving* must be physical. It involves actually moving out. The husband and wife must have their own space. The wife must have her own kitchen and her own pots and pans, so that she can cook for her husband.

The two of them now need to make their own decisions and no longer rely on their mothers or fathers to make decisions for them. Therefore they need to be mature enough to settle their own disputes. Someone said, "All the 'in-laws' are now 'out-laws." What they meant was that in-laws must leave their children to manage the affairs of their own home. The parents can no longer tell the husband or wife how to run his or her own home. Both parties can ask for advice and help from their parents, but if they don't ask for your help, parents, keep out of their affairs!

UNDERSTANDING THE INSTITUTION OF MARRIAGE

I was told about a certain mother-in-law who would go to the home of her married son uninvited and question his wife about how she was taking care of her son. She would go into her daughter-in-law's kitchen to see what kind of food she was cooking for her son and would tell her what she should cook and what she should not cook for him. She would then ask her son if he was being well fed. If you are that son, you need to let your mother know that she has no right to rule in your home. That's between you and your wife. Tell her that when you need her thoughts and opinions, you'll ask for them. Otherwise she should never come to your home to intimidate your wife. And, of course, it works the other way around as well. A man and his wife must always protect each other from invading in-laws.

Parents, there is a right and wrong time to do things for your married children. The best time for you to tell the other party about your own child is when they are in courtship or if they come and ask for your help. Then it's perfectly acceptable. Parents know their children better than anyone else. They know their likes and dislikes. So, before they get married, call them together and give them all the advice you can.

Explain to your son's prospective bride how he likes his eggs cooked or to a prospective groom how your daughter likes to be pampered, but do it during their courtship. Then, as soon as they are married, please leave them to work out their new life together. Let your daughter be submissive to her husband, and allow your son to love his wife to the best of his ability.

MARRIAGE MADE IN HEAVEN
THE CLEAVING

And Adam gave names to all cattle, and to the fowl of the air, and to every beast of the field; but for Adam there was not found an help meet for him. And the LORD God caused a deep sleep to fall upon Adam, and he slept: and he took one of his ribs, and closed up the flesh instead thereof; and the rib, which the LORD God had taken from man, made he a woman, and brought her unto the man. And Adam said, This is now bone of my bones, and flesh of my flesh: she shall be called Woman, because she was taken out of Man. Genesis 2:20-23

Adam had a beautiful garden, he had food, and he had all the animals around him, but he was alone and lonely. He had no one to cleave to. He did not have his other half. He was not a complete pair. He was like a part of the body without the rest of the body. He was alone – just a part, not the whole.

Adam had no one to cleave to, he had no one to hold hands with, he had no companion, he had no one he could communicate with verbally (except God). God saw it and said that it was not good for Adam to remain incomplete. So God gave him a helper, his other half, to complete him. Cleaving brings completion.

Cleaving meanings joining to a suitable helper. Adam was in need of help. He needed an opposite part, a counterpart or mate. He needed someone to stand beside him. None of the animals or the rest of creation qualified to fill that void. Cleaving means finding a suitable helper.

UNDERSTANDING THE INSTITUTION OF MARRIAGE

We must understand that marriage is a union between a man and a woman, not two of the same sex, or the joining of a man and a beast. You cannot marry your dog or a horse or a cat. You cannot have sex with an animal. Bestiality is a sin, an abomination to God. Christian marriage has nothing to do with any of that. Only one man and one woman qualify to cleave in the marriage union.

Today the world around us is struggling to redefine marriage, and this has gotten a lot of people confused about the issue. Marriage is and always has been a godly thing. It is a Christian thing. Therefore we cannot have the world defining it for us. We recognize that the state has its own form of marriage, and there are other religions that have their own forms of marriage, but we are talking about a Christian marriage here.

Christian marriage is being joined to a person of the opposite sex, an opposite part, not to the same sex. Christian marriage will never be same-sex. Persons of the same sex can never cleave from God's standpoint. In God's design for marriage, only opposite sexes cleave. The world may call it same-sex marriage, but God calls it sin. We are talking of marriage as God designed it, *A Marriage Made in Heaven*, not one created in man's design.

The phrase *"bone of my bone and flesh of my flesh"* equals *woman*. A man must be joined to a woman, his opposite, to complete himself and find a perfect companionship.

A man and a woman have a way of completing each other. They are built differently and operate differently, and their offices in the home are different. For example, the man naturally disciplines the children, while the woman comforts them. The man seeks to provide for his home, while the woman naturally make the house a home. The word *cleave*, according to *Strong's Dictionary* (H1692) means "to cling, adhere; figuratively to catch by pursuit: abide (fast together) follow close (hard after) be joined (together) stick." This sticking together brings a perfect union. Both bodies are naturally shaped for a perfect sexual union and for procreation.

In many cases, it is the man who first attempts to cleave to his wife. It is he who pursues the woman of his dreams. It is he who runs hard after the woman, and the woman enjoys being chased and often plays hard to get. Although some men are timid and need some encouragement, it is the man who should take the initiative. Men, if you can't read the signals, to know if a woman likes you or not, ask another woman to help you. I am convinced that it is the original plan of God for the man to pursue, to woo, to win and then to protect a woman—and not the other way around.

The woman chasing the man is new and modern. The prophet Jeremiah prophesied about it:

> *How long wilt thou go about, O thou backsliding daughter? for the* Lord *hath created a new thing in the earth, A woman shall compass a man.*   Jeremiah 31:22

A woman *compassing* a man here simply means women chasing men.

Another thing that confirms to me that it is God design that the man does the chasing of the woman, is that Christ will come for His bride, not the other way around. Do not the Scriptures say:

UNDERSTANDING THE INSTITUTION OF MARRIAGE

Whoso findeth a wife findeth a good thing, and obtaineth favour of the LORD *.*   Proverbs 18:22

The man must do the finding, not the woman.

I also believe that if the woman is the glory of the man, then he must go all out for the woman of his dreams. This brings honor to the woman.

Sex is God's design for cleaving. It is the sticking or joining together part. It is not only for the purpose of procreation and the continuity of the human race, as it is with other animals, but it is also for the pleasure of both the man and the woman. Sex was created so that they would hold fast to each other, caress each other, stick together and follow hard after each other. Solomon describes it this way:

There be three things which are too wonderful for me, yea, four which I know not: the way of an eagle in the air; the way of a serpent upon a rock; the way of a ship in the midst of the sea; and the way of a man with a maid.
       Proverbs 30:18-19

UNDERSTANDING THE ONE-FLESH CONCEPT

The Pharisees also came unto him, tempting him, and saying unto him, Is it lawful for a man to put away his wife for every cause? And he answered and said unto them, Have ye not read, that he which made them at the beginning made them male and female, and said, For this cause shall a man leave father and mother, and shall cleave to his wife: and they twain shall be one flesh? Wherefore

they are no more twain, but one flesh. What therefore God hath joined together, let not man put asunder.
Matthew 19:3-6

What? know ye not that he which is joined to an harlot is one body? for two, saith he, shall be one flesh. But he that is joined unto the Lord is one spirit. Flee fornication. Every sin that a man doeth is without the body; but he that committeth fornication sinneth against his own body.
1 Corinthians 6:16-18

For we are members of his body, of his flesh, and of his bones. For this cause shall a man leave his father and mother, and shall be joined unto his wife, and they two shall be one flesh. This is a great mystery: but I speak concerning Christ and the church. Nevertheless let every one of you in particular so love his wife even as himself; and the wife see that she reverence her husband.
Ephesians 5:30-33

These scriptures are loaded. Our Lord Jesus taught that it is in marriage that He joins a male and a female, a man and his wife, and they become *"one flesh."* Sex also serves to join them into one body. You become *"one flesh"* with the person you sleep with. God said, *"They are no more twain but one flesh"* and that no man was allowed to pull them apart. Paul said this same thing. The two become members of the same flesh and bone, and their union is similar to that of Christ and His Church. Those of us who know Him as Lord and Savior are members of His bones and of His flesh. We are the Body of Christ.

UNDERSTANDING THE INSTITUTION OF MARRIAGE

Marriage is a spiritual thing, but it is also a flesh thing. It is a compatibility and a joining of bones and flesh. Therefore, when choosing a partner for marriage, please don't be deceived. Don't tell yourself that physical appearances are not important. Body chemistry and bone structures all play their part.

For Adam's part, after considering the match, he said, *"This is bone of my bones and flesh of my flesh."* Consider your match carefully.

If you join yourself to a prostitute, you are most likely to prostitute yourself because you are now one body with a prostitute. As believers in Christ, we are also one body and one spirit with Him because we are joined with Him. Fornication (the general term used for all kinds of sexual sins) then becomes a sin because there are only two people allowed in this union. There can be no three-some and no orgy. That makes the marriage overcrowded, and God calls it sin and tells us to flee from it. By being a part of such things, you are sinning against your own body, and you are sinning against your spouse and defiling your marriage bed.

NAKED AND NOT ASHAMED

> *And they were both naked, the man and his wife, and were not ashamed.*   Genesis 2:25

If we were to take this scripture from its original meaning, we would read it like this: *"The man and his wife were nude and were not pale."* I would like for us to look at it from the point of view that they were naked, meaning that there was nothing hidden between them. The man and the woman must not be ashamed of their bodies and of exposing their nakedness to each other.

Neither the man or his wife can have any issue with being naked before each other. If you are embarrassed about anything concerning any part of your body, you need to let your other half see it and judge for themselves. If both of you are embarrassed about it, both of you need to agree as to what should be done about it.

Men are more stimulated sexually by what they see, while women are more conscious of their privacy and are stimulated by touching. Be naked and not ashamed. When was the last time you were naked and uncovered when having sex? When was the last time you had sex in the daytime or in the nighttime with a light on and the sheet off? This is important to the man as it stimulates him and gives him a greater sexual experience.

There is a higher risk for a man to be tempted to look at pornography if he cannot see his wife's nakedness. Pornography is a sin, but stop and think: could it be that your partner was drawn to it because they cannot see your naked body?

Men, assure your wife of the beauty of her body and give her confidence to appear naked in front of you. Wives, if you cannot be assured enough to appear naked before your husband, do something about it. Go to the gym or do some walking. Whatever you need to do, become confident about your body and be willing to display it to your mate.

It is good for a woman to dress in a sexually provocative way for her husband so that he will desire her. Some men are more attracted to legs, bums (rears) or breasts and some to all of the above. Know what part of your body your man is attracted to, and entice him with it. The more you draw your husband to you, the more you keep him for yourself. Don't forget that God made us sexual creatures, and marriage is the place we fulfill our sexuality.

A sister asked me once how often she and her husband should have sex. She thought that her husband wanting to have sex more than three times a week was sinful and lustful. The need for sex varies from individual to individual, so there is no one rule that fits all. It is my view that each married couple should have sex as often they are both comfortable with it. Having sex more always shows a healthy relationship.

It is an undeniable reality that a woman's body changes after giving birth and also as she ages. Illness can cause her body to change. Some medications cause weight gain, and injuries can also be a factor in her physical health. Therapy and exercise can help in many cases. Women, get the help you need. Your husband's devotion will go a long way to help you regain your confidence and get back in physical shape.

Men, face it, as we age, our bodies change, and it is unrealistic of you to expect your wife to maintain the same shape she had when you met her or when you got married. You're not getting any younger yourself. Love each other, regardless of who changes in shape and how.

Our marriage must be transparent and open, and neither the man nor the woman should have anything hidden from the other. This means that you must be transparent about past relationships. And when your mate is naked (transparent) before you, don't cause them to be pale or embarrassed. Don't be intimidated of each other's strengths, and don't embarrass each other for your lacks or failures.

Even in courtship, it is good for both parties to let the other know about past sexual relationships. This helps to prevent any unpleasant surprises in the future and can help in dealing with them.

Sex should be a time of completing each other, not of competing with each other. There is nothing wrong with saying, "I don't know how to do it." Don't just pretend to know how and then make a mess of it. Teach your mate how to please you and let him or her do the same for you.

When having sex, one should never hide their feelings. If your partner is doing something that either hurts your feelings or is physically painful, let him or her know about it. Don't say, "That's okay" when it hurts. You can be truthful without doing it in an unpleasant way. Letting your partner know they have hurt you helps them not to continue doing it or not to do it again another time. And it also helps you to not have to go through some ordeal again and again.

Be transparent when you are not deriving pleasure from sex. Letting your partner know you are hurt or that he or she is not satisfying you should not hurt their feelings, so there is no need to be afraid to let them know. If your feelings are being hurt or you are coming away unsatisfied, something needs to change. This is for the good of the marriage.

Naked (transparent) and *not pale* (embarrassed) is the theme of this section. After your other half has shared their weaknesses or failures, you should never use this knowledge against them. That is wicked. Don't be like

Delilah. After Samson had shared all his heart to her, she used that knowledge to enslave him. That is gross wickedness. When a partner exposes their nakedness, their weakness, it is so that you can help to bring a covering of healing to them, not to continue to dig on their existing wounds.

THE MARRIAGE PYRAMID

For the marriage to stand, we need to understand the order or authority in the home. When everyone finds their respective positions of authority in the Christian home, everything operates in its right order and functions as God intended.

Marriage is like a triangle. In the center of the triangle is God Himself. He should be in the center of every Christian marriage and home. Jesus is the Lord of the Christian home and family, and everything should operate under His commandments and guidelines for the home. That is a *Marriage Made in Heaven*. If there is disagreement as to how anything should be done in the home, the two need to ask: "What does God have to say about this?" Once His will is discovered, the argument ends. Both parties, therefore, must have Jesus Christ as Lord and Author of their home.

God comes first in the home and must be given the first position in everything. This means that time must be set aside to pray, to go to church and to do ministry in and out of the church.

Some time must also be set aside for abstinence from sex, so that both husband and wife can dedicate themselves to prayer and fasting:

Defraud ye not one the other, except it be with consent for a time, that ye may give yourselves to fasting and prayer; and come together again, that Satan tempt you not for your incontinency.   1 Corinthians 7:5

Every husband and wife needs God's help with being a proper spouse and a proper parent in this twenty-first century. Pray together with your spouse, and pray together with your children.

God also comes first in your finances. Paying your tithes and giving offerings must not be an option, but a rule that is carefully followed. This will ensure that your financial needs are supplied.

Adam and Eve had a perfect marriage, as long as they both obeyed God. When they were obedient to Him, they were naked and were not ashamed. After they had both sinned, Adam began to cast blame on his wife, and they both began to cover their nakedness and hide from God. When God ceases to come first in the home, there is sin, nakedness, blame and hiding.

Both you and your partner are the two equal lines meeting each other at the top of the triangle. This signifies that you are equal partners in the relationship. However, after God and serving His will, then comes the man in the relationship. The man is the head of the woman, who comes next. The children are next in line. They are represented by the line at the bottom of the triangle or pyramid:

Likewise, ye husbands, dwell with them according to knowledge, giving honour unto the wife, as unto the

UNDERSTANDING THE INSTITUTION OF MARRIAGE

weaker vessel, and as being heirs together of the grace of life; that your prayers be not hindered.   1 Peter 3:7

A man must seek to please his wife at all times and likewise the wife. When you both seek to please each other, you make a wonderful home. Put each other first. Seek each other's interest. Be sacrificial for each other and have mutual respect for each other. By love, serve each other. And beware of sin.

Your children take second place to the two of you. I always tell our children that they met their mother and me at the same time when they came into our lives, and one day they will leave us, to make their own homes. They are not to come between us:

But I would have you without carefulness. He that is unmarried careth for the things that belong to the Lord, how he may please the Lord: but he that is married careth for the things that are of the world, how he may please his wife.   1 Corinthians 7:32-33

The children are at the bottom of the pyramid. Never put your children before your partner. Woman, your husband comes before your children. Men, your wife comes first and next your children. Women, your husband is the king of your castle. Men, your wife is the queen of your castle. The children are mere princes. Never team up with your children against your partner. Your children are just passing, and your duty is to prepare them through your own example for the making of their own homes. Love your children, but love your spouse more.

It is a good practice to include maturing children in a family discussion for the purpose of decision-making in the home, but the children should understand that the final decisions are never up to them. It is the parents who are tasked with deciding what is best. Parents, make good decisions, taking into consideration how each decision will affect your children. Their interests are also at stake and that is why you should include them in the discussion, to know their feelings on a given issue.

Each partner must defend the other against misbehavior from the children. Husbands, protect your wives against misbehaving children. And the same goes for the wife. Do not tolerate verbal or physical abuse from your children against either of you. Team up and fight against it. Make a point to agree on and then enforce discipline. Never be in disagreement in the presence of your children. Show them a united force.

Children have a way of causing disagreements between their parents, but Mary and I discovered a way to stop it dead in its tracks. For example, your child comes to you and asks you if they can go out and play or if they can have ice cream from the freezer. Don't give a quick answer. First ask if they have already consulted your spouse. If they say no, then you can make your decision. If they say yes, ask them what their mother [or father] said concerning this request. Whatever has been the decision of your mate must also be your decision. If your decision is contrary, then you are showing disrespect to the decision of the other party, and you are encouraging your children to divide the two of you.

UNDERSTANDING THE INSTITUTION OF MARRIAGE

I SPEAK OF CHRIST AND HIS CHURCH

The union of a man and his wife is an illustration of the union of Christ and His Church. We are children of God. He gives us the opportunity to be like Him, to exercise His character and demonstrate His love within our human relationships. Marriage is one such opportunity. The man acts in God's stead, and the wife acts in the stead of the Church. The man is made in the image of God, and the wife is made in the image of the man. Christ is the image of God, and the Church is the image of Christ.

Unless we are able to understand this relationship and our roles, duties and responsibilities to each other we don't have a true Christian marriage. Unfortunately, there are many things couples have not been able to receive in their relationship as man and wife because they still have not understood the relationship between Christ and His Church. When you can understand this relationship between Christ and His Church and relate it to your marriage, you will have *A Marriage Made in Heaven*.

Submitting yourselves one to another in the fear of God. Wives, submit yourselves unto your own husbands, as unto the Lord. For the husband is the head of the wife, even as Christ is the head of the church: and he is the saviour of the body. Therefore as the church is subject unto Christ, so let the wives be to their own husbands in every thing. Husbands, love your wives, even as Christ also loved the church, and gave himself for it; that he might sanctify and cleanse it with the washing of water by the word, that he might present it to himself a glorious church, not having spot, or wrinkle, or any such thing; but that it should be holy and without blemish. So ought men to love their wives as their own bodies.

He that loveth his wife loveth himself. For no man ever yet hated his own flesh; but nourisheth and cherisheth it, even as the Lord the church: for we are members of his body, of his flesh, and of his bones.

For this cause shall a man leave his father and mother, and shall be joined unto his wife, and they two shall be one flesh. This is a great mystery: but I speak concerning Christ and the church.

Nevertheless let every one of you in particular so love his wife even as himself; and the wife see that she reverence her husband. Nevertheless let every one of you in particular so love his wife even as himself; and the wife see that she reverence her husband. Ephesians 5:21-33

I was already a pastor when I got married, and I have preached from Ephesians 5 many times, but I came to understand the full intent of this passage only after having been married for about ten years. We will be celebrating our twentieth anniversary on the 5th of April 2017. In the marriage union God envisioned that the man would understand and love his wife as Christ loves His Church, and the wife is to submit to her husband as the Church submits to Christ.

Today we somehow think that this word *submission* is not for the twenty-first century marriage and that the love a man extends to his wife should be conditional. I will be delving deeper into this subject later in the book, but what is important for the reader to understand in this chapter is that marriage requires that the husband love his wife as his own body, even to the point of dying for her, and the wife's submission to her husband is to be unconditional, as he is the head of the union. These are commandments given to all married people by God Himself.

Jesus left us His example:

For God so loved the world, that he gave his only begotten Son, that whosoever believeth in him should not perish, but have everlasting life. For God sent not his Son into the world to condemn the world; but that the world through him might be saved. John 3:16-17

In a sense, the husband is called to save his wife, and the wife is called to submit to and honor her husband. This specified role makes them one body, like Christ and His Body, the Church. This is the covenant that we make to each other. Christ's love for us is unconditional and eternal. It took me ten years of marriage to come to this realization.

On our 10th Anniversary, we renewed our vows to each other, and I gave Mary the greatest gift of all. I said to her, "I give you the gift of love. It is unconditional and eternal. You don't have to do anything to earn it, and nothing you can do will ever cause me not to give it. It is a gift.

"This love is given to you whether you give me sex or not. It is given to you whether you cook my food or not. It is also given to you whether you fulfill your role to be submissive to me or not. I will love you, whether you honor me or not."

Why could I say that? Why would I say that? It was because I am Christ's representative to Mary, and my love for her, therefore, is unconditional and eternal.

I also believe that submission of the wife to her husband should be done in this same way. When you (the Church) came to Christ, you confessed Him as Lord and Savior. Sarah called Abraham lord. Twenty-first century wife, your husband is your lord. Just as you submit yourself to Christ, submit yourself to your husband. Be obedient to him, as you would to Jesus. Don't be disrespectful to him. Honor him as you would honor your Lord Jesus Christ. If both parties understand these concepts, then they will have *A Marriage Made in Heaven.*

NOT EVERYONE WILL RECEIVE THIS

Jesus, as He was teaching His disciples, brought out some very profound statements concerning marriage and divorce. Although divorce is not the subject of this chapter, it would be beneficial to add at this point:

> *He saith unto them, Moses because of the hardness of your hearts suffered you to put away your wives: but from the beginning it was not so. And I say unto you, Whosoever shall put away his wife, except it be for fornication, and shall marry another, committeth adultery: and whoso marrieth her which is put away doth commit adultery. His disciples say unto him, If the case of the man be so with his wife, it is not good to marry. But he said unto them, All men cannot receive this saying, save they to whom it is given. For there are some eunuchs, which were so born from their mother's womb: and there are some eunuchs,*

UNDERSTANDING THE INSTITUTION OF MARRIAGE

which were made eunuchs of men: and there be eunuchs, which have made themselves eunuchs for the kingdom of heaven's sake. He that is able to receive it, let him receive it.   Matthew 19:8-12

Before the Law of Moses, divorce was not an option for the people of God. Moses gave them the option to divorce because they were hardened in their hearts. They could not receive this truth, just as they were not ready to receive other truths which were revealed in grace. Then the question arises: Is divorce for any reason, aside from marital unfaithfulness an option? The answer is NO! Jesus said, "...*but from the beginning it was not so.*" Moses allowed divorce under the Law, but it was never God's best.

In his first letter to the Corinthians, Paul shared some of his own views on Christians marriage. Jesus was clear: it you put away your wife, you cause her to commit adultery, and if you remarry after divorce, then you have committed adultery. The disciples were struck by these teachings and said to Jesus, "If this is the case, then it is better not to marry at all."

Jesus then made a profound statement, that not all men would receive this saying. Indeed, not all men are receiving it today. Some are receiving it, but a majority have rejected it. Not everyone can receive the idea of an unconditional marriage, without the possibility of divorce. On the other hand, not everyone can remain celibate, even for the sake of the Kingdom of God.

The truth of the matter is that marriage is difficult when one party obeys the truth of the Gospel and the other does not. It is also difficult when either or both of the parties fail to understand the truths that govern marriage. Sacrifice in such situations becomes difficult. Some have chosen to divorce and remain unmarried, while others, finding it difficult to remain unmarried, have decided it was better to remarry than to burn in lust and sexual sins. So not everyone will receive Jesus' teaching. It is only for those *to whom it is given*. God's way produces a *Marriage Made in Heaven*.

CHAPTER 4

Understanding the Importance of Agreement

LIKE ATTRACTS LIKE

Can two walk together, except they be agreed? Will a lion roar in the forest, when he hath no prey? will a young lion cry out of his den, if he have taken nothing? Can a bird fall in a snare upon the earth, where no gin is for him? shall one take up a snare from the earth, and have taken nothing at all.   Amos 3:3-5

According to this passage, the roaring of the lion has to do with food in his mouth. Something must have attracted the bird to the trap. Like attract like.

The first thing you need to understand is that there is something in the other party that attracts you to them. If you have the right kind of attraction, you can make an intelligent decision about choosing your life's partner, for you will be attracted to the right kind of person. If, on the other hand, you have the wrong kind of attraction, you will be attracted to the wrong kind of person.

The Scriptures say that Solomon loved strange women, and Samson fell in love with a woman belonging to his enemies. These were wrong attractions that cost them dearly. Marrying the wrong person or you being the wrong person for someone else to marry can cost everyone involved very dearly.

Guard yourself against being attracted to someone just because of their external or physical attributes. In choosing your life's partner, consider the total person. Physical attributes, depending on your taste of shape, color and size, are good. Popularity, fame and wealth are added blessing, but character and spirituality far outweigh them all. For example, if your choice is solely on the basis of physical appearance, what happens if the person you marry has an accident? What happens when they begin to age? Perhaps then there will be no reason for the relationship to continue. If your attraction to a man or a woman is because of money, what might happen to the relationship if he or she goes broke?

Sometimes our choice can even be wrong if we have chosen on the basis of spirituality alone. A marriage relationship is spiritual, emotional, intellectual and physical. So there must be a balance of all of these elements. You will not be praying, fasting, studying the Bible and going to church day and night. Apart from doing spiritual things together, can you interact intellectually with the person? Can you and the person interact emotionally? Are you physically attracted to this person? If you are balanced in your choice of a partner, you will enjoy your marriage. That is *A Marriage Made in Heaven* because God made us all spirit, soul and body, and every part of us has needs that must be fulfilled within the proper context.

PREPARE FOR IT

> *For which of you, intending to build a tower, sitteth not down first, and counteth the cost, whether he have sufficient to finish it? lest haply, after he hath laid the foundation, and is not able to finish it, all that behold it begin to mock him, saying, This man began to build, and was not able to finish.*   Luke 14:28-30

If you cannot take the time to carefully consider the type of partner you will choose in marriage and, together with that partner, agree on the kind of marriage you want, you won't have a marriage worthy of your expectations. Somewhere in the building process things are bound to crop up that have the potential to destroy your marriage. During courtship, sit down and talk.

Talk about how many children you wish to have and how you can reconcile that with your career and income? Talk about how you want to raise your children? Where do you intend to live? Find out if your prospective spouse is in sync with your dreams? What are your priorities in your marriage? What can you afford to compromise, and what can you not afford to change for any reason? All of these questions and more should be thought of, discussed and agreed upon before considering marriage.

Don't shove anything under the carpet, thinking that everything will somehow fall into place when you have entered into marriage. Marriage is not a magic act that put everything in place. And love is not blind. Love sees into the future and makes provision for it. If you wait until you get married, only to discover that you have irreconcilable differences, then your marriage is over. You could have saved yourself and the marriage time by discovering these things in advance, when you were still in the courtship stage and would not have gotten married in the first place. Trying to build a foundation after you have put up the entire building is folly? Know what kind of house you are building, and then lay a proper foundation for it:

> *And every one that heareth these sayings of mine, and doeth them not, shall be likened unto a foolish man, which built his house upon the sand: and the rain descended, and the floods came, and the winds blew, and beat upon that house; and it fell: and great was the fall of it.*
> Matthew 7:26-27

Most people take seriously the need to lay a proper foundation for their desired career. After all, that career represents their future livelihood. So we study and research, take exams and whatever else is required, and then, once we have entered in that career, we work hard to advance it.

We pay a heavy price for our career, sacrificing and making time for it. How sad that we fail to put even a fraction of that same effort into building a lasting relationship with our spouse or would-be spouse. Many actually spend more time preparing for their wedding than they do preparing for their marriage.

UNDERSTANDING THE IMPORTANCE OF AGREEMENT

The all-too-common thought: "If marriage doesn't work, I can always pull out," must be eradicated from the minds of people who want to be part of the institution of holy matrimony. Both parties must go into the marriage with the attitude: "I will give it all I have to make it work." The vows we repeat during the marriage ceremony say just that:

"It must not be entered into lightly or unadvisedly but reverently and in the fear of God."

This should be the foundation of every marriage.

If your would-be spouse cannot sit down with you before the marriage is consummated and plan together the life you hope to share, that is a flashing red warning light that this building you are trying to build will never stand. If the two of you cannot talk about it and plan for your home during courtship, no magic can make your marriage workable.

LET'S TALK FIRST

To be fair, I believe that people do talk about what they want for the future. The problem is that one party often refuses to listen, or they cannot understand each other's "language." We send signals all the time, whether we know it or not.

One day a lady was walking in the street with sporty shorts that fit her so well that her curves made a dent in her shorts, which ended just short of her curvy butt. A man who was driving was attracted to her bum and said to her, "Lady, do you know what I could do with that butt?"

In this exchange, both parties communicated. One was a verbal communication, and the other was non-verbal. The woman sent a signal, and the man responded.

The point is this: the way you dress talks. It can say, "Hey, look at me; I'm sexy" or "I'm traditional" or "elegant" or "natural" or "sporty." The next communication from this man driving by was: "We could have good sex." Her body had attracted him, and he thought it would be good for sex. The truth is that far too many relationships today are based on little more than sex. Sexual attraction is good, but if the relationship is only based on sex and there is no understanding the true meaning of sex within the Christian context, that relationship is built on a faulty foundation.

A sister caught her partner having inappropriate flirting conversations with other women on a social network, so she confronted him with the issue. He first denied it, but when she showed him the proof, he apologized and promised not to do it again. When she caught him a second time, his defense was that it was nothing, just the way he and the other girls communicated.

The woman insisted that these conversations he was having with other women were inappropriate, while he continued to insist that it was nothing. He then refused to speak of it again, but he continued doing what he was doing.

His next effort to justify himself was to try to make his partner feel that she was somehow the one with the problem, so he began to accuse her of being "insecure" and of "making much ado about nothing."

We must never let unresolved issues die. Never stop communicating in a particular area if the other party is not

UNDERSTANDING THE IMPORTANCE OF AGREEMENT

satisfied or settled in the matter. This man had a problem he was unwilling or unable to admit. He was in denial and was casting the blame on the innocent party. Therefore this woman had a decision to make. Should she go ahead with her planned marriage to this man? Was it possible to get him to change his ways? Or should she let go of this relationship and move on? Unfortunately many go into marriage with unresolved issues that later turn around and bite them. If your partner cannot change his or her ways during courtship, there is no guarantee that he or she will change once you have marry him or her—ever!

Courtship is a time for the would-be couple to talk about everything. They need to talk about spiritual things, about money and how to handle it, about children, about sex and everything else that pertains to marriage. They should ask each other questions and leave no stone unturned. This leaves no room for future surprises. Where there is a disagreement, there must be compromise.

After receiving all the information and processing it, you can then decide if you can take what you have into marriage or not. Don't wait to talk until after the marriage. After marriage there is nothing to talk about. You have already entered into a binding contract. Many marriages should not have happened in the first place, hence many divorces could have been prevented—if the couple had first dialogued well in their courtship.

You need to know this person's sexual history (good or bad). You need to know the other's views about sex. You need to ask about the other's views, for example, on anal sex, three-somes, etc. If things arise that you know your Christian belief does not allow you to participate in, then you need to reconsider whether you want to marry such a person or not. You don't want to be married and have your partner bring in someone else to share your bed with you. (It may surprise some readers to know just how far "Christians" can go these days sexually. Let it be known that Christians should never be bisexual, homosexual or lesbian.)

Before the marriage, both parties need to be tested for STDs (sexually transmitted diseases). These days, you also want to know if the person you are considering for marriage might have had a sex change or if this person "feels trapped" being "a man in a woman's body" or the other way around. You don't want to get yourself into a relationship where the other party cannot reproduce because they don't have a womb.

If she is a woman, has she removed her womb for any reason? If he is a man, is he perhaps sterile? Love is not blind. Love sees whether you are about to be taken advantage of or not. Ask about everything. The stakes are too high.

Wherever possible, ask to see your prospective partner's medical history. If you have any doubts or suspicions about what you see there, clear up those doubts and suspicions by asking the right questions. Don't be deceived by your partner insisting, "Don't you trust me?" Answer that you are building a proper foundation for trust. That's what courtship is all about.

If someone wants to marry you, then it's up to them to give you the information that can build a foundation for trust. They must prove themselves worthy of trust. Trust is not given; it must be earned. Don't end up berating yourself and asking yourself why you have been such a fool. Don't just date! Court, and do it properly!

In this way, you can enter the marriage knowing exactly what you are getting yourself into. It does not hurt to ask questions; it hurts not to ask questions. Investigate the person thoroughly, and do it before you take any other steps toward marriage. Seek the opinion of other people who know the person you are considering as a future mate. Then you can make your own judgment. Make a list of things you want to bring up, and then don't be afraid to ask them all.

One couple had been married for more than ten years when one day a day a girl came knocking at their door asking for her dad. The husband had not told his wife that before they were married he had a daughter by another woman. When the wife asked him why he had not told her, he said: "The subject never came up." That was very big information to keep secret, don't you think? So ask your prospective mate if they already have children. You don't want any surprises to foul your marriage.

THE IMPORTANCE OF COURTSHIP

In my view, a Christian should never go on a date. Dating may be for the world, but courtship is for the Christian. Any and every relationship with the opposite sex, for a Christian, should be entered into with the intention of it leading to marriage. Christians have no business having relationships for the purpose of sowing their wild oats, practicing sex or testing the case. You wouldn't want anyone practicing on you or testing you in this way, as if you were some sort of experiment, so don't do it to others.

Also, in Christian courtship, it is inappropriate and rather ungodly for a brother or sister to be "seeing" more than one person at the same time.

THE NEEDED PRAYERS

> *Ask, and it shall be given you; seek, and ye shall find; knock, and it shall be opened unto you: for every one that asketh receiveth; and he that seeketh findeth; and to him that knocketh it shall be opened. Or what man is there of you, whom if his son ask bread, will he give him a stone? Or if he ask a fish, will he give him a serpent? If ye then, being evil, know how to give good gifts unto your children, how much more shall your Father which is in heaven give good things to them that ask him?*   Matthew 7:7-11

It is my advice to all who want to get married to start praying in their choice of partner early in life, even if they are not yet ready for marriage. Sow much prayer into your marriage beforehand, and you will save yourself a lot of grief in years to come. Ask the Lord to help you make the right choice in this regard. Take the time to pray about it, and pray about it often. Many want a good Christian relationship, but they have taken no time to pray for it.

Many sisters dress up and put on make-up to attract brothers. They flirt, and they try to get through to the "man's heart through his belly," but they seem to have no time to pray for God to help them in their choice. Unfortunately today Christian women go to the extreme of showing a prospective partner how good they are in bed and are even prepared to get pregnant for their partners,

UNDERSTANDING THE IMPORTANCE OF AGREEMENT

thinking they can hook him, in this way, into the relationship, by having a child for him. How unfortunate and unwise! Too often these schemes backfire and the woman ends up being hurt and disappointed. Your heavenly Father knows you have need of a husband or a wife, so please pray before you go seeking for Mr. or Miss Right. Your persistence in prayer will open the door for you. Wait on God, He does not disappoint. The Scriptures admonish:

In all thy ways acknowledge him, and he shall direct thy paths.   Proverbs 3:6

The question many times asked is this: "Is there only one man for each woman?" Meaning has God created a specific woman for a specific man. The wrong answer to this question has caused many problems in marriages today. Some, in fear that they have made the wrong choice, live their entire lives in regret, sure that they are "out of the will of God" in their marriage. If things are not working in their relationship, for whatever reason, they go further by saying that God is punishing them as a result of their wrong choice of a partner. They are sure that their troubles are a consequence of their disobedience to God for their bad choice of partner.

Others say that they married out of the will of God, but they have now found the will of God and, "to please Him," they have divorced the person they were married to, in order to marry the one who, they are sure, is the will of God for their lives. I used to hold to the belief that there was only one particular man for a particular woman, that God had ordained, for example, that Sister Jane marry Brother John, but I no longer hold that belief. Instead, I believe that there are several people who could fit each other. Allow me to tell you why I no longer hold that belief.

First, if there is only one man for one woman, if the man makes the wrong choice and marries someone else, he has left the "right woman" without a partner. I don't think that the justice of God would allow your "wrong choice" to leave someone out there without a life partner. I can't believe that your wrong choice would affect the will of God for someone else's life.

Secondly, what would happen to someone who had made the right choice, but their partner died? If there were only one right man for each right woman, the only right choice for this life would now be dead, and they would not be able to remarry because the only right person for them on earth would be gone.

Many people have made their choice of marriage partner when they were still unsaved, so they no longer need to pray for a partner, as they are doing fine with their choice. Many later get saved and their partners get saved with them, and they are doing fine. Paul even teaches that if one partner is later saved and the other is not, and the unsaved party wants to stay with their partner, the saved person should not divorce them:

> *But to the rest speak I, not the Lord: If any brother hath a wife that believeth not, and she be pleased to dwell with him, let him not put her away. And the woman which hath an husband that believeth not, and if he be pleased to dwell with her, let her not leave him.* 1 Corinthians 7:12-13

UNDERSTANDING THE IMPORTANCE OF AGREEMENT

The Bible does not teach, in any form, that God has made a particular man for a particular woman. There is no scripture that says this, so it is a wrong idea, and it is bringing about guilt in many homes and is the cause of many divorces. Christians are leaving their married partner for another, saying that they married "the wrong person." This does not eliminate the fact that people do make wrong choices in life. I'm just pointing out that the idea that one particular person is only right for another particular person, in my own view, is untrue.

Paul talks about marrying *"whom she will; only in the Lord."* This, I believe, refers to marrying a believer, one who is in the Lord, as you are, and doing it with the Lord's guidance:

> *The wife is bound by the law as long as her husband liveth; but if her husband be dead, she is at liberty to be married to whom she will; only in the Lord.*
> 1 Corinthians 7:39

NOT BEING UNEQUALLY YOKED

> *Be ye not unequally yoked together with unbelievers: for what fellowship hath righteousness with unrighteousness? and what communion hath light with darkness? And what concord hath Christ with Belial? or what part hath he that believeth with an infidel? And what agreement hath the temple of God with idols? for ye are the temple of the living God; as God hath said, I will dwell in them, and walk in them; and I will be their God, and*

they shall be my people. Wherefore come out from among them, and be ye separate, saith the Lord, and touch not the unclean thing; and I will receive you, and will be a Father unto you, and ye shall be my sons and daughters, saith the Lord Almighty. 2 Corinthians 6:14-18

A Christian, in every sense of the word, should not enter into courtship or marry anyone who is of another faith or anyone without faith. Christians should not marry Muslims, Hindus, Sikhs or anyone of any other religion, regardless of how fine or moral or how good his or her family background is. The Bible says clearly, *"COME OUT from among them and BE YE SEPARATE."* This refers to any such relationships, which the Bible describes as an *"unclean thing."*

Also please know that not all who go to Church are true Christians. Prove a person before you enter into any sort of relationship with them. *"By their fruits you shall know them,"* the Bible says. If your partner in courtship is taunting you and pouncing on you, in an attempt to have sex, believe me that person is not saved. How can I say that? If their treatment of God and His Word is that casual, they are not saved. If the fear of God is absent from their life, they may have religion, but they don't have true salvation. They are not a new creature. They are the same old, same old, they are carnal by nature, and they are sinners—pure and simple.

I understand that a person can be tempted once or twice to sin and can then come back to their real, true Christian sense, but someone who is willing to live in fornication is not saved.

UNDERSTANDING THE IMPORTANCE OF AGREEMENT
I WILL CONVERT HIM

It is unfortunate that women go into a relationship with an unbelieving person with the idea that they have some kind of power to convert them, either in the courtship or in the marriage. Believe me, you cannot convert anyone. The power of conversion is not in your hands. It is in the hands of our Lord Jesus Christ and the power of the Holy Spirit. It is also in the willingness of the person to accept salvation.

Believe me, if he or she really loves you, they will get converted first. Although getting married is not a reason for someone to get converted (the true reason for conversion is the conviction of sin and the need for repentance and faith in Christ for salvation), I have seen a beautiful situations where it worked.

A certain lady came to know Christ. She had been living with a Muslim man, and they had children together, but the man refused to marry her. We advised her that if her partner would not marry her, then she must leave him. She took her children and left, in obedience to her faith in Jesus to *"flee fornication"*:

> *Flee fornication. Every sin that a man doeth is without the body; but he that committeth fornication sinneth against his own body. What? know ye not that your body is the temple of the Holy Ghost which is in you, which ye have of God, and ye are not your own? For ye are bought with a price: therefore glorify God in your body, and in your spirit, which are God's.*
>
> 1 Corinthians 6:18-20

In time, she met a young man at a party, and he fell in love with her. When he confessed his love to her, she told him that she was a Christian and would not enter into a relationship with any non-believers. He said he loved her and wanted to marry her, and if it took him being converted to Christ, he was willing to do that.

"Well," she said, "if you are serious about marrying me, you need to come and see my pastor." He said that was not a problem.

The man came to see us, and the result was that he gave his life to Jesus Christ as Lord and Savior. He married the sister, even after knowing her previous situation and that she had children by another man. To make a long story short, that couple is still married today, and the man is now senior pastor of one of the largest churches in Sierra Leone. He still loves his wife just as much as he did the first day he laid eyes on her, God has blessed them with more children, and they are all in the house of God.

What is the moral of this story? If your partner is not willing to get saved, dump him or her like lead in the ocean. Two cannot work together unless they agree and, as far as religion is concerned, they both need to be of the same faith.

Many believers are struggling with their Christian lives today and in their marriages because they have married an unbelieving person or someone of another faith. Those who are going out with unbelievers have compromised their faith. This compromise causes their relationship to be just like that of an unsaved couple. Constantly they live in fornication because they want to please the unbelieving partner. They compromise with their partner to get drunk, go to wild parties and even take drugs. Then they live in constant guilt for their hypocritical lives. Some eventually backslide, being converted by their unsaved partners, instead of them converting their unsaved partners to God.

Many Christian women marry Muslim men and fall into a trap. Even though the man has said to them, at the first, that he does not mind them being Christian, after the marriage, they are then forced to become Muslim. Afterward, their husband then takes a second wife, and they have to start living with a roommate in the home. They are told either that a woman does not have a religion or that they should adopt the religion of their husbands. They are then forced to say Muslim prayers, fast for Ramadan, etc. In some of these families, the man himself is more liberal, but his parents force the issue, and he has no choice but to comply.

The moral of the story is: Don't marry a Muslim. It is not worth the suffering you will endure. God's laws are always for our good, not His own. Obey them and you will be happy.

Any marriage, in itself, is hard work—understanding each other, learning communication skills, learning how to please each other sexually, providing for the family, taking care of the children, etc. Therefore eliminate any unnecessary conflicts in your marriage, and don't add unnecessary pressures to it.

THE IMPORTANCE OF WATCHING

Watch and pray, that ye enter not into temptation: the spirit indeed is willing, but the flesh is weak.   Matthew 26:41

No one knows you better than you know yourself. God said of Adam, *"I will make him an help meet for him"* (Genesis 2:18). You know who is suitable for you. With God's help, you can make a proper decision. Someone said that marriage is not just about finding the right partner, but also about being the right person for the other party. You will eventually know the person who is suitable for you.

As you pray about finding your suitable help meet and are led to someone, begin to observe that person. God will not give you someone you are incompatible with. If you cannot stand someone, he or she may not be the right person. It does not have to be 100% compatibility, but in my judgment, 70% compatibility and over is acceptable.

Observing and praying must be done simultaneously. If you see that someone is getting close to you, or you feel yourself drawn to someone, begin to ask the Lord about that person, and then start observing the person. But keep praying. Both prayer and observation must go hand in hand. It's called "watch and pray."

We all usually know our physical preferences in a man or a woman. If you have not taken the time to know yourself, stop and understand your likes and dislikes and the kind of personality and physical attraction you might have. Begin to take inventory, and God will help you.

It's funny, the way we were brought up in this Christian faith. Among certain groups of Christians, the thought is that the more unattractive and unkempt a person is the more he or she is the will of God for you—"as long as she loves the Lord dearly." In this type of church, attractive-looking sisters who really take care of themselves are presented as Jezebels, even if they do love the Lord, and if

UNDERSTANDING THE IMPORTANCE OF AGREEMENT

you're in interested in them, you are considered to be lusting after beauty. Some even think that good-looking sister cannot possibly love the Lord, that she is a deception.

In some settings, ministers of God are taught that nothing else matters in the attributes of their future partner except for how useful she could be to their ministry. Skills or giftings like singing, playing a musical instrument or whether she is an intercessor, Sunday school teacher or in children's ministry, or an evangelist are what needs to be considered in the choice of a sister for marriage. In this context, she is only being considered as a help or enhancement to your ministry. If this is true, then choosing a partner for a pastor is only a case of career development. If she can't do any of these things, then she's not pastoral material.

All of the assets can be a blessing to a pastor, but they should never be the only reason he chooses a certain woman for his spouse. A spouse like that might be married to your ministry and not necessarily married to you. This also could be the reason for marital unfaithfulness and many divorces among Christian ministers today. Far too many ministers today have wives who are only good for public show and the status it brings. At home, they fight like cats and dogs, and there is no bone-of-my-bone and flesh-of-my-flesh connection between them. Their home life is a disaster that will soon enough show itself in their public life.

Believe me, you want a partner who is married to you. Your partner can be a suitable help to you in certain areas of ministry. But for the sake of the marriage and then the family, when children, come, she needs to be a good administrator, a good housewife, a good travelling companion, a good encourager. She needs to be good at organizing your finances and investing your money.

Marry because you love someone and because the two of you are compatible in many respects, not just for career reasons. Just because you are a doctor doesn't mean that you have to marry another doctor. There may well be advantages to the two of you having the same occupation, advantages like being in the same circles and having the same things to talk about, but let that not be the only reason for your marital union.

The story is told of a young minister who was faced with the choice of marrying one of two different young ladies in his church. One of them could sing like an angel, but she was very unfortunate in facial beauty. The other was just a homey type, with no special skills for ministry, but she was very beautiful. The young man was advised to marry the one who could be more profitable for his ministry, so he chose the singer and they were married.

When the young pastor woke up the first morning of their honeymoon and looked over at his bride, he was struck by how unattractive she was, and he was filled with regret. Her ungainly face was entangled in the sheets and she was rumpled with sleep, making her even more unattractive to him. He shook her from her sleep and said to her, "Honey sing! Sing! Please sing!" He was seeking for consolation through her singing voice.

Facial beauty cannot be the only factor we consider when seeking a mate, but you must realize that you will be seeing that face for many years to come, not only on your partner, but also on the children for generations to come.

UNDERSTANDING THE IMPORTANCE OF AGREEMENT

THINGS YOU SHOULD LOOK FOR

Man is a tripartite being, meaning that there are three sides to us. Man is a spiritual being, a soul being and a physical being.

Every part of a man has needs, and ignoring one of the parts and its need can cause that person to be tempted to abnormal behavior. A Christian spouse or a Christian seeking a spouse must consider all aspect of the other person.

EXAMINING THE SPIRITUAL ASPECT

Is your partner a Christian? Is he or she saved? Does he or she have a relationship with Jesus Christ of Nazareth? Is Jesus Christ the Lord of their lives? Is he or she regular at prayer meeting and Bible studies? Is he or she a member of a church? Are they faithful in tithing? Do any of the pastors know him or her to belong to that church? Is he or she involved with any of the various groups in the church?

How committed is this person to God and how highly does he or she regard the Word of God? Does he or she take God and the things of God lightly or casually? Does this person respect his or her leadership? Does this person have personal devotional time with God on a daily basis?

All of these questions are very important. If the person does not have a spiritual foundation, he or she will not understand the significance of the marriage union. The relationship between a wife and her husband is the same relationship that Christ has with His Church. If both parties are not spiritual enough to understand this, there can be no proper foundation for their marriage.

If your partner has no respect for the Bible, he or she will have no respect for its values. If Jesus is not the Lord of their lives, they will find no need to obey Him. If they don't have respect for their pastor, they will not respect his counseling. If they are not committed to their church, they will not bring up their children to do likewise.

If this person is not committed to church attendance, they will not grow spiritually, so don't compromise the spiritual values of the person of your choice. If that person does not have them, he or she is not an acceptable candidate for courtship, let alone marriage. This is the foundation and without it there is no marriage. Get firmly planted on this foundation and you have a *Marriage Made in Heaven*.

Chapter 5

Understanding the Need for Compatibility

Compatibility is a word often used when speaking about marriage partners, and nothing could be more important. Refuse to marry anyone you are not compatible with.

What kinds of character or personality are you tolerant of or intolerant of? Can you tolerate people who are loud, self-willed, boastful, proud, talkative and nagging? Can you tolerate people who are bashful and quiet? Everyone has his or her own taste in character. Don't go for the character you detest, and don't think you can change someone overnight. Marriage is not about making your partner the way you want him or her to be. It is about being right for each other at the start.

During courtship is the time you must begin to look into your likes and dislikes. It is a time you get to know each other better. It is a time you decide whether this is the kind of person you want to take into marriage. There are things both parties may not like about each other, but as you communicate about your dislikes and show your willingness to change and compromise with each other, you will make progress in your relationship. If one party is not tolerant to change, then it won't work. Never forget that two cannot walk together unless they agree.

Do you like his or her choice of colors, dress ethics, and friends? Do you like his or her family? Share honestly what you don't like about each other and discuss how these things might be remedied. Some people are embarrassed by certain things about their prospective spouse, but not wanting to hurt their feelings, they refrain from telling them anything about it. If you love your partner and want to be proud of them in public and in private, you have to let them know their faults.

I don't mean embarrass your partner. Instead, admonish them. For example, your partner might have a bad body odor. A person who is a good friend will tell this, and the other should receive it in good faith.

If you have problems with your partner's relations or friends, don't say, "I won't be marrying his [or her] family or friends, but him [or her]." Family and friends influence relationships a lot. These people have been in their lives before you came on the scene, and they can be strongholds you never imagined. If a person's family and friends are not happy with the choice of partner, this unhappiness will eventually affect your marriage.

I'm not saying that you need to please your partner's friends and family. I'm just saying that if your spouse is embarrassed before them because of you, that can affect your home. A dialogue with your partner, to look into these things and to arrive at a conclusion pleasing to both of you, is necessary.

UNDERSTANDING THE NEED FOR COMPATIBILITY

One sister told her partner that her mother came first in her life, even if she got married to him. "Mummy has always come first," she told him. Well, the brother could not have Mummy controlling his home, so the relationship came to an end. Another sister told a friend who was becoming close to her that her pastor would come first in her life, even after she was married. The end of the story is that she eventually married the pastor.

FRIENDSHIP COMPATIBILITY

Mary was my friend before she became my wife. Many people today frown at the idea of their partner being their friend. They say, "You are my friend, so I can't marry you?" That is a very big mistake! A friend is someone you trust, someone you tell about your day, and someone with whom you share similar interests. A friend is someone on whose shoulder you can cry and share your burdens with.

You don't pretend to your friend. Your friend knows when you are sad, happy, lying or telling the truth. Your friend knows what you are capable of doing and what you are not capable of. A friend stays with you when you fall and when you rise. Who else would you like to spend your entire life with, if it's not a friend?

> *A man that hath friends must shew himself friendly: and there is a friend that sticketh closer than a brother.*
>
> Proverbs 18:24

Husbands and wives should be best friends. It is amazing when people marry and yet have someone else as their best friend. That's crazy!

Many couples can't communicate with each other or settle their differences because they're not friends. That's why a third-party friend ends up breaking up their home. If you don't share the same interests and have nothing to talk about, then there is no friendship. Do you really know your partner? Are they a mystery to you? Marriage is a mystery enough. Please don't add more mystery to it.

One day I was listening to an interview done with a man who had been married for more than fifty years. One of the things, he said, that had kept them together all those years was that his spouse was his best friend. He said that now that they were older, they had ceased to be sexual lovers, but their friendship had remained. They always had things to talk and laugh about.

Friendship is what keeps a marriage, and friendship can keep you home and keep your home in tact. If the two of you have nothing in common, don't even continue the courtship. And please don't marry that person because your marriage might well be a very lonely one.

THE IMPORTANCE OF PHYSICAL COMPATIBILITY

Someone has said that Christians can be so spiritually minded that they are of no earthly good. This can be true in marriage. Marriage is a physical union of a man and a woman. Whether you want to think of it that way or not, the fact still remains. Marriage is a sexual thing, and physical chemistry is involved. Sex is not only for the purpose of bearing children; it is also for the pleasure of the couple involved:

> *Marriage is honourable in all, and the bed undefiled: but whoremongers and adulterers God will judge.*   Hebrews 13:4

UNDERSTANDING THE NEED FOR COMPATIBILITY

Everyone has physical attractions. Being a Christian does not mean that Christ has killed your physical attraction to someone for marriage. You know the kind of physical body that is sexually appealing to you. Many Christians go into marriage on the guise that physical beauty does not matter to them. They only marry for spiritual reasons. But those types end up in a mess because they neglect the physical attraction and fail to fulfil their physical needs. They later disclose that they could not stand their spouse and started looking elsewhere to satisfy their physical needs, and all of this made a mess of their marriage.

If I just wanted a prayer partner, there were many people I could have prayed with in the church. If I just wanted to evangelize I could have joined an evangelistic team. When I get home and my flesh needs a soulmate, I'm not looking for an intercessor. I need a sexual partner, someone who is romantically appealing to me. At that moment, I don't need a sister because I don't sleep with my sister. I want a wife, a bone of my bone and flesh of my flesh. It is not wrong to fulfill all the spiritual dots. Do that, but remember to tick off the physical dots too.

You know whether you like a tall or short person. You know your preference of skin color, shape, bust, and hips etc. I do not apologize for being so graphic here. Solomon, in the book that was his song, was extremely graphic. He knew what was sexually appealing to him, and he described his lover's lips, neck, hair and on down to her breasts.

God created you a sexual being, and to be sexually satisfied by your spouse is good. It keeps your eyes off that secretary or personal assistant, choir leader and dancer in the church or your neighbor's wife. It is not balanced having all spirituality at home and no physical attraction. Many who have married just for the sake of status or to please their parents, are not sexual attracted to each other at all.

Unfortunately, this is the plight of many marriages today. Sex with the marital partner is a struggle. When they eventually get up their courage to have sex, even as they are doing it, they are thinking, "Let's get this done with quickly, so that I can get out of here." Some, as they are having sex with the partners, have to imagine that they are having it with someone else. This is all a result of not considering well before marriage and marrying someone you are not physically attracted to.

THE BIBLICAL POETRY OF LOVE

Mr. and Mrs. Spiritual tell me I am carnal for talking like this, but I will tell you that sexual behavior is both spiritual and carnal. Let's look at King Solomon's poem of love:

> *Let thy fountain be blessed: and rejoice with the wife of thy youth. Let her be as the loving hind and pleasant roe; let her breasts satisfy thee at all times; and be thou ravished always with her love. And why wilt thou, my son, be ravished with a strange woman, and embrace the bosom of a stranger.* Proverbs 5:18-20

Isaiah recorded these words:

UNDERSTANDING THE NEED FOR COMPATIBILITY

Rejoice ye with Jerusalem, and be glad with her, all ye that love her: rejoice for joy with her, all ye that mourn for her: that ye may suck, and be satisfied with the breasts of her consolations; that ye may milk out, and be delighted with the abundance of her glory.   Isaiah 66:10-11

Solomon continued:

A bundle of myrrh is my wellbeloved unto me; he shall lie all night betwixt my breasts.
My beloved is unto me as a cluster of camphire in the vineyards of Engedi.
Behold, thou art fair, my love; behold, thou art fair; thou hast doves' eyes.
Behold, thou art fair, my beloved, yea, pleasant: also our bed is green.
The beams of our house are cedar, and our rafters of fir.
       Song of Solomon 1:13-17

Thy two breasts are like two young roes that are twins, which feed among the lilies.
Until the day break, and the shadows flee away, I will get me to the mountain of myrrh, and to the hill of frankincense.
Thou art all fair, my love; there is no spot in thee.
       Song of Solomon 4:5-7

Thy two breasts are like two young roes that are twins.
Thy neck is as a tower of ivory; thine eyes like the fishpools in Heshbon, by the gate of Bathrabbim: thy nose is as the tower of Lebanon which looketh toward Damascus. Thine

> *head upon thee is like Carmel, and the hair of thine head like purple; the king is held in the galleries.*
> *How fair and how pleasant art thou, O love, for delights! This thy stature is like to a palm tree, and thy breasts to clusters of grapes.*
> *I said, I will go up to the palm tree, I will take hold of the boughs thereof: now also thy breasts shall be as clusters of the vine, and the smell of thy nose like apples;*
> *And the roof of thy mouth like the best wine for my beloved, that goeth down sweetly, causing the lips of those that are asleep to speak.* Song of Solomon 7:3-9

> *We have a little sister, and she hath no breasts: what shall we do for our sister in the day when she shall be spoken for.* Song of Solomon 8:8

Women and men alike have their physical preferences. They like good smells, the way someone walks, dresses and goes about doing things. God created you a sexual being. He gave you sexual desires, to be satisfied within the context of marriage. So why not find the one you can enjoy sharing that gift with? Yes, these references are graphic, but if you cannot feel that way for your partner, please reconsider before you enter into marriage. If not, God forbid that you do find yourself embracing the breast of a strange man or woman.

CONSIDERING FINANCIAL COMPATIBILITY

> *A feast is made for laughter, and wine maketh merry: but money answereth all things* Ecclesiastes 10:19

UNDERSTANDING THE NEED FOR COMPATIBILITY

Money, wealth and fame should never be a motivation for marriage. I know that financial security is very important to a woman, but wealth should never be her only motivation. These days money can buy a lot of things. Money can even buy someone to marry you. In a Christian marriage, please do not put money first. There are people who will marry your money, but not you.

A lady in London fell in love with a gentleman and wanted to marry him. This happened at the time of his greatest financial struggle. She, on the other hand, had a house and a car, and she was a manager in a company, so she had money enough for both of them.

The man, however, refused to marry her, telling her that he was not in love with her. She called him "stupid" and said that she could have given him all that he could have ever dreamed of. "He was kicking away his own blessing," she concluded.

The man said he wanted her to be happy so he had told her the truth. Someone else, he insisted, might have married her, taken all that she had, and then left her heartbroken. He was right. Please don't try to buy a person into marrying you. The person who can love you and make you happy may not be as financially strong as another. Many women have accepted financial security with a man but have not found happiness, even in the midst of their newfound affluence.

Women, it *is* important that your intended married partner be employed. He must have a source of income before you get married. If he does not have a job, wait until he has one before you marry him. There are many lazy men who want their partners to take care of them financially. There are also lazy women who just want to live on men. They have no interest in contributing financially to the wellbeing of the home. They want you to meet all their needs, and they are not even homemakers.

If a man is still staying with Mum and Dad, he does not pay bills, and has no job, please dismiss him as a candidate for marriage. He is a boy, and he needs to become a man before he can marry. If a sister does not have a pot in her house and cannot cook or take care of her room, please look elsewhere. That woman is not ready for marriage. I am sorry, but twenty-first century women still cook and wash clothes and dishes.

When you are in courtship, if the other party doesn't want you to pry into their affairs, they are not ready for marriage yet. There should be no skeleton left in the closet, no secrets left undisclosed. If he or she has money, property, child support or debt anywhere, you want to know about it. You want to know if this person is bankrupt or has debts because when you marry him or her, you inherit their debt, and you don't want any surprises.

OTHER AREAS OF COMPATIBILITY

Courtship is a time for talking, praying, and observing each other, taking a stand, making compromises in areas that are not steadfast, helping each other through weaknesses and building each other to the place of marriage. So there is a lot to talk about during this period. A good marriage does not just fall from the sky, and you cannot just sit around thinking that everything will fall into place by itself. No! A good marriage comes to people who work for it.

You need to talk about your sexual dispositions, although some may not have discovered it yet. At least you

UNDERSTANDING THE NEED FOR COMPATIBILITY

have an idea. A sexually cold person cannot live with a sexually hot person. You need to talk about children and agree if you want any and how many.

In these days of affluence, the man often owns a house, and the woman also has her house. You need to talk about where you will live. Whose house will be your residence? Traditionally the man takes the woman to his house, but it is up to the couple to decide this.

If you are from different churches, you need to talk about church. Traditionally, since the man is the priest of his house, he takes his wife to his church, but they have to discuss this and decide. This (and other decisions) may not be easy. At the end of the day, the final decision belongs to the man.

We had a problem in the first church I pioneered in London. The husband of one of our most faithful sisters was not a part of our church. He insisted that she join him in his church, but she refused to attend or join his church. Though I hated letting the woman go, I had to tell her that her place was with her husband. I prayed for her and sent her on her way. Pastors need to be careful not to cause problems in marriages in such by trying to hold a member back.

PLANNING AHEAD

Courtship is a time to plan ahead. You can plan your ministry, your education, your career, your children, your finances, etc. It is a time to look at where you want to be financially for the first year of your marriage, your first five years, then ten years, then your retirement plans. Planning is very important. You are two builders building a house. Someone said, "If you fail to plan, you have planned to fail." In fact, the whole issue of courtship is about planning. At whatever point the two of you feel that you are right for each other, that's the time to begin to plan your future together. And please don't break your plans. Be dedicated to see them through to the end.

HOW LONG DO I COURT?

The Bible does not specify any precise time that a courtship should last. My courtship with Mary was for six months, and after that we got married. I must start by saying that courtship is not for primary or secondary school children. It is for people who are not a long way from getting married.

Many have messed up their courtship by living in fornication. They have unwrapped and used their Christmas gift before Christmas, so to speak. They could not wait. Keep your courtship pure, and don't keep it too long because it is better to marry than to burn with lust.

Here are some practical steps to keep you pure and to avoid sinning:

- Always spend time praying for your relationship and pray that God keeps you pure.
- Never stay late at night at your partner's home. (When I was in courtship with my partner, now my wife, I gave myself no later than 10:00 PM.)
- Never spend time together in the bedroom with the doors shut. Always make sure the doors are open when you are together in a room.
- Never sleep over at your partner's house.
- Keep yourself from sexual touching.
- Always try not to be alone in the house.

UNDERSTANDING THE NEED FOR COMPATIBILITY

These steps may seem old-fashioned and out of date, but they will keep you from sinning and keep your relationship pure. The long and short of it all is that you must have the fear of God in your relationship, and God says that no fornicator shall enter the Kingdom of Heaven. This helped us keep our relationship pure until we married, and it will do the same for you.

Esau could not receive the blessing because he was a fornicator. You do not know what blessing may pass you by because of the sin of fornication:

But now I have written unto you not to keep company, if any man that is called a brother be a fornicator, or covetous, or an idolater, or a railer, or a drunkard, or an extortioner; with such an one no not to eat. 1 Corinthians 5:11

Lest there be any fornicator, or profane person, as Esau, who for one morsel of meat sold his birthright. For ye know how that afterward, when he would have inherited the blessing, he was rejected: for he found no place of repentance, though he sought it carefully with tears.
Hebrews 12:16-17

Flee fornication. Every sin that a man doeth is without the body; but he that committeth fornication sinneth against his own body. What? know ye not that your body is the temple of the Holy Ghost which is in you, which ye have of God, and ye are not your own? For ye are bought with a price: therefore glorify God in your body, and in your spirit, which are God's. 1 Corinthians 6:18-20

BE CAREFUL ABOUT MATCH-MAKING

I don't believe in match-making, although many pastors I know do. There is no right or wrong to it, but it is just not my practice. You might think you know all about the two people involved and how well they could fit each other, but you could also be wrong. Parents can be good at finding the right mate for their children, having known them from birth, but parents can also be selfish and can choose for financial security and social status reasons. Consider very objectively the advice of your parents and pastors. Dialogue with them, but then take it all to the Lord in prayer before making a decision.

I believe it's fine for parents and friends to introduce two people in friendship and let them get to know each other, but eventually the two of them must make their own decision without undue influence from others. If you introduce someone, let them know that they are under no pressure to choose that particular party as their life companion and that you are just introducing them as friends.

We also have to be very careful these days about the match-making being done through so-called "prophetic words." Don't blindly obey such a prophetic word and marry someone without God also speaking to you personally to confirm it. If you receive no confirmation, don't go ahead with it. It is your life, and God has to speak to you as well. If you are having difficulty hearing from God, ask the Lord to confirm His will through another source, for by the mouth of two or three witnesses every word will be confirmed.

HOW CAN MY CHURCH HELP?

Many churches have put together programs of various kinds to help their young people build strong relationships.

UNDERSTANDING THE NEED FOR COMPATIBILITY

The purpose is to help to minimize unnecessary hurt and to prevent sin. Some programs have been good, and others have not. It is good for churches to have guidelines, and I want to give an example of such guidelines. I also want to tell you what we have done in our own church. If your church doesn't have such a program, this might encourage you to design and implement one.

First, I want to point out that this church is a community-based church with married people and also celibates. This is how the program works: If a brother, after praying, believes that a particular sister is a choice for him, he must first talk to his shepherd about it (and he also prays about it). The shepherd also may offer his opinion as to whether or not he thinks that particular sister could be a right choice for that brother or not.

The next step is for the shepherd to approach the sister and ask her if she also has been praying about having a relationship, and, if so, if there is anyone special in her heart? If she calls the name of the brother in question, then this is considered to be a confirmation. If, on the other hand, she has no one in her heart, she may be asked to pray about this particular brother and come back to report her feelings to the shepherd. This may be a yes, or it may be a no. If there is a confirmation, then the relationship starts, and regular counseling begins.

There is nothing wrong with you asking your pastor or another leader in the church to pray with you in the area of relationship in your life. He is your shepherd, so he can offer prayers and give you counsel, especially if the other party is from the same church. If the other party is from another church, your pastor will be able to communicate with the other pastor and get details to help you with a decision.

When two people are in courtship, it is only appropriate that their relationship be made known to the leaders of the church. This is important because the church can give them valuable guidance.

In a small church, the pastor or an assigned elder can attend to courtship matters among the members. As a church grows larger, however, there should be a marriage and home pastoral team to look after these things. I recommend that couples in courtship be assigned to a counseling leader in the church, someone who can guide them through their courtship period and be in prayer for them until that courtship eventually ends in marriage.

Unfortunately, not all courtships end in marriage. That spiritual leader must also be taught how to heal wounds if and when a courtship ends in separation. Relationships must have a foundation of love, honesty, truth and trust. Unfortunately this does not prove to be the case in many relationships, and they end in a shambles. When these things happen, we all need to lend our support to get the wounded back on their feet. Always remember God's intention. It is that you have a *Marriage Made in Heaven.*

CHAPTER 6

Understanding What Love Is

It is amazing how different our perceptions are of what love is and how we must express it. It might amaze you to know some of the bizarre things people think love is. If your perspective on love is different from that of your partner, you are heading for trouble. Since God *is* love, I would like us to see what He has to say about this subject. If we love God's way, we will find common ground, and there will be no misconception about the subject.

Some of the various viewpoints on love are:

1. **The controller's view**: "If you don't do what I tell you to do, you don't love me." They always try to make the other party feel guilty if they don't do as they have requested.
2. **The over-feeder's view**: Those who show their love for you by stuffing you with food
3. **The jealous view:** Those who feel that they must be jealous of anyone of the opposite sex who comes near you, to make you know that they love you. They feel that if they don't show signs of jealousy it indicates that they don't love you. Some also feel

that you have to show signs of jealousy to prove to them that you love them.

4. **The sadistic view**: A woman was complaining to someone that her husband did not love her. She was asked why she felt this way, and she replied that her husband had never quarreled with her or beaten her. She felt that her husband should show his love for her by being jealous to the extent of beating her. This is sad. There are other sadistic views like this, and some are even more weird.

5. **The sex view:** Those who feel that love can only be expressed through sex. They feel that if they show you how good they are in bed you must know for sure that they love you. Unfortunately, when they meet the wrong person, they only use them for sex. There are relationships in which a partner cannot be introduced to friends or relatives, and the couple cannot go out together during the day. There only purpose for being a couple is for sex.

6. **The gifts view:** Those who think that love is getting your partner to lavish you with gifts or vice versa.

7. **The given birth view:** (the oldest of all) women who think that if they give birth to a child for a man, he will love them and stay with them. Unfortunately, that's the reason we have so many single parents today. Leah thought that by giving birth to sons for Jacob he would love her, but his love was for Rachael:

And Leah conceived, and bare a son, and she called his name Reuben: for she said, Surely the Lord *hath*

UNDERSTANDING WHAT LOVE IS

looked upon my affliction; now therefore my husband will love me. Genesis 29:32

It is usually the case that if the man loves his child's mother, he will also love the child, and it he hates the child's mother, he might also hate the child.

The Bible mentions three kinds of love. I believe every one of them is necessary in a proper marriage relationship.

AGAPE

Agape is the God kind of love. This love is unconditional. It is the love God has for the Church and the love a husband must express toward his wife and the wife toward her husband. Agape is love until death, and this is the vow the husband and wife make in marriage: "Till death us do part." This is the love that gives, but not on the basis of what it receives. It is the love one gives in spite of what he or she receives. Jesus, on His cross, was receiving spite and abuse, but He still loved His tormentors. This is the love we are called to express in marriage.

But God commendeth his love toward us, in that, while we were yet sinners, Christ died for us. Romans 5:8

We must express our love for each other, even if and when we are not getting love from the other party. We must love each other in spite of our shortcomings and failures.

> *[Love] beareth all things, believeth all things, hopeth all things, endureth all things. Charity never faileth.*
>
> 1 Corinthians 13:7-8

This kind of love does not fail. It wins over the heart of even your enemies. It is the love of God that bears all things. It is the love that forgives all things and hopes all things. It gives without sparing. It is longsuffering and behaves kindly. Let your love be unconditional in your marriage. Love the God-kind of way.

> *Charity suffereth long, and is kind; charity envieth not; charity vaunteth not itself, is not puffed up, doth not behave itself unseemly, seeketh not her own, is not easily provoked, thinketh no evil; rejoiceth not in iniquity, but rejoiceth in the truth.* 1 Corinthians 13:4-6

PHILEO

The second kind of love is called *phileo*, from which the word *Philadelphia* comes, meaning "brotherly love." This is family love, the love a father would have for his children or, similarly, the love the children would have for their parents. It is the love siblings have for each other. This is deep-rooted affection for a family relation. We also need phileo love in the marriage, for we are brothers and sisters as well as husband and wife. We must love each other as such.

David had phileo love for Jonathan and he grieved for Jonathan, his friend and covenant brother, at his death. This was an expression of his brotherly love for his friend:

UNDERSTANDING WHAT LOVE IS

O Jonathan, thou wast slain in thine high places. I am distressed for thee, my brother Jonathan: very pleasant hast thou been unto me: thy love to me was wonderful, passing the love of women. How are the mighty fallen, and the weapons of war perished. 2 Samuel 1:25-27

EROS

Eros is the erotic kind of love. It is the love a husband should have for his wife and vice versa. It should not be misunderstood for infatuation or lust. Unfortunately, many are consumed with lust, and they think it is love. Sexual love must only be shared with one partner.

This is not a sex book, but I would like us to look at some principles or guides to sex in light of the Scriptures (and my personal opinion about the matter):

Nevertheless, to avoid fornication, let every man have his own wife, and let every woman have her own husband. Let the husband render unto the wife due benevolence: and likewise also the wife unto the husband. The wife hath not power of her own body, but the husband: and likewise also the husband hath not power of his own body, but the wife. Defraud ye not one the other, except it be with consent for a time, that ye may give yourselves to fasting and prayer; and come together again, that Satan tempt you not for your incontinency . 1 Corinthians 7:2-5

PRINCIPLES FOR CHRISTIAN SEX

I believe that these guidelines can make the covenant of sex pleasurable and healthy within the Christian home.

MARRIAGE MADE IN HEAVEN

I also believe that these principles will help avoid hurt and pain within the Christian marriage and make sex honorable and undefiled. Here are some of them:

NO THIRD PARTIES

In the Christian context, sex should never be a threesome, nor polygamous or bigamous; neither should there be any mistresses or boyfriends in its union. If there is a third party, then that marriage is overcrowded. Sexual love is sacred and must be thought of as such. It should only be done within the confines of the marriage covenant, only between the two parties.

NO PAIN INFLICTING

Sexual love must be aimed at pleasing each other and not pleasing oneself at the expense of the other. It should never inflict pain but, rather, bring pleasure. It should be for the pleasure of both parties. It should be done when both parties are ready for it and should not be abusive or sadistic.

NOT UNILATERAL

You should not force your partner to do anything they are not comfortable doing, and what you are requesting from your partner you, too, must be willing to give. It must be mutual. It must be aimed at pleasing each other and climaxing each other.

A wise man will ask his wife how to please her, and a wise woman will do the same. Anything that is not comfortable to either party should be discussed, and personal convictions must be taken into consideration.

UNDERSTANDING WHAT LOVE IS

That is why sex needs to be discussed before marriage. If you discover that you would not be able to please the sexual desires of your partner and that there should be no compromise, then don't marry that person. It's as simple as that.

NOT TO BE DEFILED

God created sex for two main reasons: (1) For the procreation of the human race and (2) For intimacy and pleasure within the confines of marriage. Here are some ways it can be defiled:

- When sex is engaged in outside marriage, it is the sin of fornication.
- When it is done with someone else's marriage partner, it is the sin of adultery.
- When it is done with an animal, it is the sin of bestiality.
- When it is done with multiple exchanged partners at the same time, it is an orgy, and that also is a sin.
- Having sex with a same-sex partner is homosexuality or lesbianism, both of which are perversions of sex, according to the Word of God.

Everything in the marriage context needs to be talked and worked at, including sex. Couples need to talk about when they want to have children, how they want to space their children, and the preparations for unplanned pregnancies.

They need to talk about using contraceptives and understand their functions. You want contraceptives that prevent pregnancy, not ones that kill the babies. If you don't believe in contraceptives, you have to prepare for unplanned pregnancies. In many cases, it is the woman who employs the contraceptives, so she has to choose which ones are best for her.

Couples also need to talk about how they can improve their sexual relationship. Learning to communicate and understand body language when having sex is a very important part of this. You need to understand when your partner is enjoying sex and when they are uncomfortable for any reason. Keep doing the things that your partner enjoys, and stop doing things that make them uncomfortable. If you don't make these adjustments, sex will not be something they look forward to.

SETTING THE STAGE

The proper setting and a change of scenery is often important to improving our lovemaking. Discovering new positions also can help to make sex more exciting. One lady put it this way, "You can get tired of eating rice and beans every day." In this context, she was talking about always having sex in the missionary position.

How do you handle the situation if one party becomes uninterested in sex or if the man begins to have erectile problems? No one, when they get married, expects to have problems like these, so it is important to know how to deal with them if and when they arise.

The truth is that sexual disfunction is not uncommon, and some married couples have to deal with it or risk losing the glue that holds them together. The most important thing is to lovingly talk about the situation. If you do, you

UNDERSTANDING WHAT LOVE IS

can always find a way to resolve it. Love always finds a way. Be supportive of each other.

CREATE ANTICIPATION

An important part of setting the stage for sex in marriage is to anticipate or expect it. Promise yourself and each other you will have sex, and then look forward to it. Give each other a call during the day and tell each other how much you are looking forward to your intimate time together. That anticipation is good and will keep you running home to each other.

PROVIDE PRIVACY

The Bible calls your sexual organs "secret parts." The most common terminology in English-speaking circles is private parts. They are not secret or private to each other, but from the rest of the world. Genesis says, *"And they were both naked, the man and his wife, and were not ashamed"* (Genesis 2:25). Your bodies are for each other, but Christians never practice public sex or sex in an open space. Both parties must make sure that their intimacy is exclusive to them only and not viewed by others. Couples also need to be careful about their children butting in on them when they are having sex. If your children are home, please make sure your bedroom door is securely shut when you are having sex and also when you are sleeping naked.

Children never see parents as sexual beings, even though they know their parents have sex. They see us as mums and dad, and that's what we have to be before them. It is permissible for them to see us being affectionate to each other, but not to see us having sex. It is also not advisable to allow children to hear your groans of delight. They will not understand them.

Because it is best to have sex in a relaxed atmosphere, all necessary precautions must be taken with aforethought. Even if you just want to have "a quick one," don't let down your guard when children are around. Keep your intimacy private.

A CHANGE OF SCENERY

Sex can be done anywhere you choose in the house. Some people are traditional and only want it in the bedroom, in the bed and at night with all the lights off. In time, however, that can become boring. If so, change your scenery. Take an occasional weekend in a hotel, have sex in the shower, in the bathtub or even in the living room. Try using scented candles or colored light bulbs. Keep your time together exciting by making some changes from time to time. Try covering your bed with rose petals or having some grapes or other desirable fruit or cheese at your bedside to share. Whatever you need to do, keep your intimate time together exciting.

THE NECESSARY FOREPLAY

Husbands, woo your wives. Pet her, kiss her, caress her, and get her ready. Don't just jump on her and start having straight sex. Only penetrate her when she is ready, enjoy it together, and climax together. This makes sex beautiful and pleasurable and creates a *Marriage Made in Heaven*.

CHAPTER 7

Understanding Your Roles, Functions and Responsibilities

THE ROLES OF THE HUSBAND

The husband is the head of the home, just as Christ is the Head of the Church, so his task is great and his responsibility is heavy. He has to understand the role of Christ to the Church and then to function as head of his home. Here are some important points to remember:

HONOR YOUR WIFE

Likewise, ye husbands, dwell with them according to knowledge, giving honour unto the wife, as unto the weaker vessel, and as being heirs together of the grace of life; that your prayers be not hindered.   1 Peter 3:7

Even though the Bible speaks of the husband honoring his wife, this subject of honor must be mutual in the marriage. Why is the husband singled out for special attention here, in what capacity is he to honor his wife, and what are the consequences if he fails to do so?

The Bible answers that the husband should honor his wife:

1). Because she is the weaker sex, and
2). Because they are heirs together of the grace of life.

BE THE PRIEST OF THE HOME

The husband must be a spiritual man, for he is to be the priest of his house. He is Christ's representative in his home and, therefore, must be spiritually responsible. He is the savior of the body. He must make sure that the spiritual life of every member of the family, including his own, is in tune with God. He is the Bible teacher in his home, the intercessor, the one who makes sure his family serves and obeys the Lord. Therefore, he must love the Lord and must teach his family to do the same. This responsibility is reflected in the teaching that is often misused:

And if they will learn any thing, let them ask their husbands at home ... .   1 Corinthians 14:35

In days of old, it was the husband who acted as priest in the home, offering the sacrifices for the whole family, and it is still true today. A Christian husband must make sure that his family goes to church, pays tithes, etc. In Old Testament times, Elkanah made sure each of his wives and their respective children had their portions to take to the house of the Lord on the feast days (see 1 Samuel 1:4-5) He must pray for his wife and children.

A Christian husband must organize family prayer and Bible study times for his family. The Scriptures tell us that Rebecca was barren, but Isaac, her husband, prayed

UNDERSTANDING YOUR ROLES, FUNCTIONS AND RESPONSIBILITIES

for her, and she gave birth to twins. Many husbands put their wives away because they cannot bear them children. Husbands should pray for their wives to conceive and give birth:

And Isaac was forty years old when he took Rebekah to wife, the daughter of Bethuel the Syrian of Padanaram, the sister to Laban the Syrian. And Isaac intreated the LORD for his wife, because she was barren: and the LORD was intreated of him, and Rebekah his wife conceived.
Genesis 25:20-21

One of the reasons why God chose Abraham was that He knew Abraham was a man who would teach his children and all his household the ways of the Lord:

For I know him, that he will command his children and his household after him, and they shall keep the way of the LORD , to do justice and judgment; that the LORD may bring upon Abraham that which he hath spoken of him.
Genesis 18:19

BE THE PROVIDER FOR THE HOME

The husband is the designated breadwinner of his home, and he must provide food and shelter for the whole family. He must clothe his wife and children. He must provide for his family's total financial wellbeing, and not doing this is shown in scripture to be tantamount to denying the faith.

But if any provide not for his own, and specially for those of his own house, he hath denied the faith, and is worse than an infidel.   1 Timothy 5:8

There may be times when a man may be between jobs, and the woman must be willing to help out in such circumstances and still maintain her position of submission to her husband.

I believe that it is God's will for the husband to provide salvation for his family (that which the household can be sustained by), even as Christ provides salvation for His Church (that which His Church should live by). As the Scriptures say, He is the Savior, or provider, for the body.

For the husband is the head of the wife, even as Christ is the head of the church: and he is the saviour of the body.   Ephesians 5:23

Since we are now living in the twenty-first century, someone might say: "Husbands and wives both work now, so all financial responsibilities should be shared equally." Even in Bible days, when husbands provided the principal income sources for the home and the women stayed home and raised the children, this didn't mean that they contributed nothing. Looking to the classic example of the virtuous woman of Proverbs 31, we can see that she did many things that contributed to the family welfare.

The fact that a woman works and earns does not free her husband from his defined role as family breadwinner. She is his helper, so he can let her go as far as she is comfortable with toward making a financial contribution. That doesn't make him less of a man or change his role or responsibility in any way.

Because the woman has so many other duties in the home, the husband should never impose financial responsibility on her. She must be free to decide how far she wants to go and can go to support the family. The rest is his responsibility.

BE THE LOVER

The Scriptures are categorically clear that the husband should love his wife to the extent of being willing to die for her, even as Christ died for His Church. A husband should live and die loving his wife:

> *Husbands, love your wives, even as Christ also loved the church, and gave himself for it; that he might sanctify and cleanse it with the washing of water by the word, that he might present it to himself a glorious church, not having spot, or wrinkle, or any such thing; but that it should be holy and without blemish.* Ephesians 5:25-27

A husband must love his wife and, by loving her, help her overcome her faults and weaknesses. The first love a man must have for his wife is the *agape* love — God's unconditional love. That love goes beyond her faults and nurtures her to be holy and faultless. Christ died, not only to save us, but His love also nurtures us to spiritual growth and Christian maturity. Loving and nurturing your wife with the Word of God will make her a glorious wife, one you can praise and adore.

The husband's love for his wife must also be *phileo*. He must have a brotherly love for his wife. God is her Father, just as He is your Father, so she deserves your care and protection. She is family, so she deserves respect. She is a joint heir with you of the grace of life.

Your wife is under the protection of God, her Father, so if you don't treat her right, you risk God not answering your prayers:

> *Likewise, ye husbands, dwell with them according to knowledge, giving honour unto the wife, as unto the weaker vessel, and as being heirs together of the grace of life; that your prayers be not hindered.* 1 Peter 3:7

The husband, as lover, must be a romantic man, and he must give romantic pleasure to his wife. The duty of the husband in the marital bed should be centered on how he can please his wife (and, likewise the wife on how she can please her husband). The husband must provide whatever pleases his wife. That is a lover's duty:

> *But he that is married careth for the things that are of the world, how he may please his wife.*
> 1 Corinthians 7:33

> *... but she that is married careth for the things of the world, how she may please her husband.*
> 1 Corinthians 7:34b

Husband and wife need to please and satisfy each other because it is their marital right, and, therefore,

UNDERSTANDING YOUR ROLES, FUNCTIONS AND RESPONSIBILITIES

their obligation to do so. The only time God say that they should be apart is when they mutually consent to devote themselves to prayer and fasting:

> *Let the husband render unto the wife due benevolence: and likewise also the wife unto the husband. The wife hath not power of her own body, but the husband: and likewise also the husband hath not power of his own body, but the wife. Defraud ye not one the other, except it be with consent for a time, that ye may give yourselves to fasting and prayer; and come together again, that Satan tempt you not for your incontinency.*   1 Corinthians 7:3-5

The husband, as lover, must prepare the way for romantic love. He must lure and woo his wife to bed. To accomplish this, he must show himself to be romantic. He may bring home flowers for her, buy her something she has been wanting, or whatever else it takes to set the stage for love:

> *Therefore, behold, I will allure her, and bring her into the wilderness, and speak comfortably unto her.*
>   Hosea 2:14

BE THE FINAL DECISION MAKER

As the head of the home, the husband is the final decision maker (see 1 Corinthians 11:3 and Ephesians 5:23). Everyone must consult with him before any final decision is made. I call him the "consultation decision maker" and never say that he is "the decision maker," because there are far too many decisions to be made in a given home for him to make them all. He often gives managerial control over the family to an astute wife. But if she is the manager, then he is the managing director.

Managing directors often call their managers together to get from them all the information they need to make a final decision on a given matter. In the meantime, the managers under them are free to exercise their authority, within the guidelines set by the director. A good husband will always consult with his wife before making any major decisions.

Being a man does not give a husband the right to make unilateral decisions regarding the welfare of the whole family. Every couple should have mutually understood guidelines in place for decision-making, and both should honor those guidelines.

Have family business meetings to discuss what needs to be done in the home, what needs to be bought for the home, when this should be done, and what falls where in terms of family priorities. This is just good home management, and this is how Mary and I have always done it.

I might come up with an idea, and Mary and I both might like the idea, but we will often have differing views on how it should be done. When this happens, I ask her to give me her reasons for doing it her way, and I give my reasons for doing it my way. Then, I have to weigh it all and make a final decision. Sometimes I do what she has suggested, and sometimes not, and sometimes we can meet in the middle and make it work. It's always good when everyone wins. What is important is that my final decision be fair to all concerned and for the general good of all, and not for some selfish ambition of my own.

UNDERSTANDING YOUR ROLES, FUNCTIONS AND RESPONSIBILITIES

There are times when children can be included in such a discussion, but they need to understand that, in the end, the final decision belongs to Dad. The decision I take might work well, or it might not. If it works well, then the whole family will benefit, and if it fails, all will suffer. This shows how important our decisions are.

With the understanding that decision-making is never easy and is not a science, when Dad's final decision does not work, there must be understanding all around. Your idea might not have worked any better.

BE THE PROTECTOR AND DEFENDER

The man is the protector of his home, and his wife and children look to him to defend them. He is to protect them to the point of laying down his life for them—if necessary. He must protect them from his own relatives or friends who might like to take advantage of them or disrespect them.

Protection also includes financial security, so he must protect his family from a culture that would allow his relatives to take everything he has away from his family in the event of his untimely death. He must prepare and sign the necessary legal documents to make sure this doesn't happen. Your "next of kin," the person who will inherit from you, should be a member of your immediately family, not a relative.

Protection includes discipline. Although both parents should discipline their children, usually it is the husband who ends up doing the most of it. It is a biblical calling:

Train up a child in the way he should go: and when he is old, he will not depart from it. Proverbs 22:6

For whom the L{\small ORD} loveth he correcteth; even as a father the son in whom he delighteth.   Proverbs 3:12

The father who corrects and disciplines his children protects them from future trouble. Correction keeps them from the foolishness that could destroy them. Of course, such correction must be done *"in the fear and admonition of the Lord"* (Ephesians 6:4) and not in a provocative way.

THE ROLES OF THE WIFE

The wife also has her duties, as part of this covenant relationship. She is the wife, and as such, she comes second in the relationship, as the helper to the man. If she fulfills her role as the man does his, they can both find fulfillment in the marriage. But marriage only works when two believers in Jesus obey Him as Lord over their marriage, when they know their defined roles and perform them to the best of their ability.

BE HIS FAITHFUL HELPER AND COMPANION

And the L{\small ORD} God said, it is not good that the man should be alone; I will make him an help meet for him.
     Genesis 2:18

The greatest challenge of the twenty-first century home is who helps whom and who's boss. The wife is to help the man provide for the home, although she is not the chief provider of the home. The wife is to help the husband fulfill the divine mandate given to him by God and help him to maximize their full financial potential.

UNDERSTANDING YOUR ROLES, FUNCTIONS AND RESPONSIBILITIES

There is nothing wrong with a woman having a career of her own, but there is everything wrong with her being a career woman. Let me explain. First, you are a woman, and your first duty is being a woman. If you have a career, that career should not interfere with you being a woman. And a career cannot totally displace your other roles in the home.

BE THE HOMEMAKER

The wife is to be the homemaker. Proverbs 31:10-31 gives us a lot of interesting points concerning her homemaking activities: She works with her hands, she prepares food for her house and decorates it. She is business minded, for she sews dresses, plants vineyard, etc. In short, she is domesticated. She tends to her role as homemaker.

I realize that cultures are different and, therefore, this could be applied in very different ways in different places. But the principles are still the same. I would encourage every man to investigate the cooking and housekeeping skills of any would-be wife long before you actually marry her. If you are a traditional man, make sure you have a traditional wife. If you are contented not to have a woman who can cook or is not otherwise domesticated, then you will have to decide how you and your children are to be fed, who will do the laundry, who will clean the house, etc.

When the wife is employed and help out with financing the home, then it is only right for the man to help her with the traditional household chores. Work out between you what each one will be expected to do.

WHERE LOVE IS, ROLES ARE SHARED

Lot's of compromises can be made where love is, depending on the situation each partner finds themselves in. For a time I worked from home and Mary worked away from the home. It was up to me to help her with shopping, the cooking and the cleaning and I did that until our circumstances changed. When both parties are in love, if one party is not able to do everything needed in the home, the other part needs to be ready to step in and do it. Where love is, roles are shared because the home is one. Where there is no genuine love, parties take advantage of each other.

Every home goes through changes in circumstances, therefore partners must work in support of each other where and when the need arises. Just as the husband is the designated bread-winner of the home, in the same way the wife is the designated homemaker of the home, according to the Scriptures. The general rule is that the wife should be submissive to her husband, and the husband must love his wife. The wife comforts the children, while the husband disciplines them. These all should be done to meet each other's needs and as a means of expressing love to each other.

One husband may not mind his wife fulfilling certain roles, while the same might be a problem with another husband. Role-sharing must be discussed during courtship, especially in areas where circumstances might change in the home.

Wives, submit yourselves unto your own husbands, as it is fit in the Lord.   Colossians 3:18

UNDERSTANDING YOUR ROLES, FUNCTIONS AND RESPONSIBILITIES

HONOR YOUR HUSBAND

The wife's role is also to honor her husband. She must honor him in public, before their children, and in private. This means that she must be respectful to him. The King James Bible even uses the word *"reverence"*:

> *Nevertheless let every one of you in particular so love his wife even as himself; and the wife see that she reverence her husband.* Ephesians 5:33

This means respecting him, noticing him, honoring him, venerating him, preferring him, esteeming him, praising and admiring him. God knows what each of us needs. A wife needs to be loved, and a husband needs to be respected. If we give each other what is due to the other, then our marriages will be blessed.

We need to understand that our duties to each other are more than just duties to each other. They are also God's commandments to us, and no one is allowed to break God's commandments under any circumstances whatsoever. Your obligations as husband or wife were not given to you by your spouse. These are God's commandment to each of you. You cannot say, "Because my other half has disobeyed God, in not fulfilling his [or her] role, I can also disobey Him." You cannot say, "Because my wife did not submit to me, I don't have to love her anymore." No! Two wrongs do not make a right.

> *For after this manner in the old time the holy women also, who trusted in God, adorned themselves, being in subjection unto their own husbands: even as Sara obeyed*

Abraham, calling him lord: whose daughters ye are, as long as ye do well, and are not afraid with any amazement.
1 Peter 3:5-6

SUBMIT TO YOUR HUSBAND

Wives, submit yourselves unto your own husbands, as unto the Lord.   Ephesians 5:22

Therefore as the church is subject unto Christ, so let the wives be to their own husbands in every thing.   Ephesians 5:24

The wife's commandment from God is to be in submission. In other words, her first reflex must be to obey her husband. The husband is as Christ in the home, and his wife is as His Church. The husband's duty is to lead his family into the will of God for their lives, and the wife needs to submit to that.

Again, what a husband may accept in his home will be totally different from another husband in his home. Your submission as wife is to your own husband and not to someone else's. For example, one couple may agree that the wife work and the husband be a "househusband," or the husband may do all the cooking. After they have discussed it and the husband agrees to it, that's okay for that family. Another husband may decide that the role of cooking is for the wife, so she must stick to her role.

Everything about the home should be the subject of discussion, but the final decision is the husband's, and whatever he decides, the wife must be in subjection to it, according to the will of God.

The woman generally raises the children, although the man helps a lot in the process. In our very busy societies these days,

UNDERSTANDING YOUR ROLES, FUNCTIONS AND RESPONSIBILITIES

both parents must do their part, filling in where needed to care for the children from cradle to their teenage years. Mothers need help with feeding their babies, changing diapers (nappies), making school runs, parent-teachers' meetings, and attending school plays and sports events, etc. Do it all with a heart of love:

> *But let it be the hidden man of the heart, in that which is not corruptible, even the ornament of a meek and quiet spirit, which is in the sight of God of great price. For after this manner in the old time the holy women also, who trusted in God, adorned themselves, being in subjection unto their own husbands: even as Sara obeyed Abraham, calling him lord: whose daughters ye are, as long as ye do well, and are not afraid with any amazement.*
> 1 Peter 3:4-6

The Scriptures speak of the wife putting on an ornament of a meek and quiet spirit and says of such a spirit, *"which is in the sight of God of great price."* Women, God wants you to dress for your husband. He wants to see you wearing ornaments of a meek and quiet spirit.

Your meek and quiet spirit will be a product of your trust in God. That trust is that if you do your part, then your husband will perform his duties toward you and make the right decisions for your home. Your meek and quiet spirit is a reflection of your submission and obedience to your husband, as unto Christ Himself. Sarah was obedient to the point of calling her husband lord. Such a spirit is a reflection of Christ and of His Church. A Christian wife is a daughter of Sarah, and she will do well to behave like Sarah.

The meek and quiet spirit God calls for is just the opposite to a raging, abusing, cursing and disrespectful spirit toward your husband. Being meek and quiet shows confidence in your faith in the Lord, without fear that your husband will make the right choices, choices that will not bring your home to the gutter. This does not mean that you should not speak or express your thoughts in any matter. What is does mean is when you speak your truth and make your point, you do it in a meek and quiet spirit. This comes across to a man much better than raging at him:

> *My son, hear the instruction of thy father, and forsake not the law of thy mother: for they shall be an ornament of grace unto thy head, and chains about thy neck.* Proverbs 1:8

> *The rod and reproof give wisdom: but a child left to himself bringeth his mother to shame.* Proverbs 29:15

Depending on the society, if a child is not brought up well, the blame usually goes to the mother. From the biblical standpoint, the woman is also key to the upbringing of her children. Children must be taught to obey their parents in the Lord because it is the right thing to do. It is also a commandment that comes with a blessed promise of longevity. Fathers are warned by God not to provoke their children to wrath, but to bring them up in the nurture and admonition of the Lord (see Ephesians 6:4). Nothing could be more important if you really desire a *Marriage Made in Heaven*.

Chapter 8

Understanding How to Properly Divide Your Time

TIME FOR GOD

Man was created in the image and likeness of God. He is the glory of God and, as such, is the priest of his family. He should, therefore, be responsible for the time his family needs to dedicate to God. The man must make sure his family is in church, pays their tithes, and is involved in church activities. He must make sure he and his family have family devotions, and he must be in constant prayer for his wife and children. God said of Abraham:

> *For I know him, that he will command his children and his household after him, and they shall keep the way of the* Lord *, to do justice and judgment; that the* Lord *may bring upon Abraham that which he hath spoken of him.*
>
> Genesis 18:19

Many husbands today blame their wives for everything, just as Adam blamed Eve for giving him the forbidden fruit to eat. I cannot say that husband are responsible for all of the misbehaviors of their wife, but some of these could be avoided if husbands were constantly in prayers for their wives as Christ is for His Bride, His Church.

Jesus is always at the right hand of God the Father interceding for His Bride. Jacob prayed for his wife Rebecca to give birth when she was barren. Today we see men divorcing their wives because they cannot give birth. Some women suffer threats, cursing and even physical abuse from their husbands because they cannot give birth for them. This is not the answer; the answer is to pray for your wife:

> *And Isaac intreated the LORD for his wife, because she was barren: and the LORD was intreated of him, and Rebekah his wife conceived.* Genesis 25:21

Husbands and wives need to take time together for spiritual retreats, just as they do for a second, third or fourth honeymoon. The Scriptures talk about husbands and wives giving themselves *"to fasting and prayer"*:

> *Defraud ye not one the other, except it be with consent for a time, that ye may give yourselves to fasting and prayer; and come together again, that Satan tempt you not for your incontinency.* 1 Corinthians 7:5

TIME TO WORK

Husbands and wives must both be hard-working people because running a home costs money. They must work in order to eat and also to live well, save well and

UNDERSTANDING HOW TO PROPERLY DIVIDE YOUR TIME

invest well. When needs are not met in the home, there are frustrations on every side. When there is no money, many times there is trouble. Poverty and poor money management wreck many marriages and destroy many homes.

There will be times when cash may not flow as is desired, but as long as the two have a solid work ethic, they are bound to succeed. One member can be in full- or part-time education, or they might just start a ministry or business that is not yet bringing as much money as it should, but this is only for a time. It is difficult when there is no plan for money to come in, and one (or both) partners does not want to go out to find a job to make ends meet. Take heed to the warning of the Scriptures:

> *For even when we were with you, this we commanded you, that if any would not work, neither should he eat. For we hear that there are some which walk among you disorderly, working not at all, but are busybodies. Now them that are such we command and exhort by our Lord Jesus Christ, that with quietness they work, and eat their own bread.*   2 Thessalonians 3:10-12

> *Go to the ant, thou sluggard; consider her ways, and be wise: which having no guide, overseer, or ruler, provideth her meat in the summer, and gathereth her food in the harvest. How long wilt thou sleep, O sluggard? when wilt thou arise out of thy sleep? Yet a little sleep, a little slumber, a little folding of the hands to sleep: so shall thy poverty come as one that travelleth, and thy want as an armed man.*   Proverbs 6:6-11

TIME FOR PLAY

Hard work and wise money management pay off. You will be able not only to pay the bills, but also to save for a rainy day, make some investments and even have something left over for a time of pleasure together. It is good for a family to have a vacation time, when Dad, Mum and the children can all have a fun time away from home. It is also good for Mum and Dad to have occasional times apart by themselves. At such times, they will need to get someone to take care of the children.

During normal times, it is good to get the children to bed at their bedtime, so that the two of you can spend some quality time together. By spending time together, I mean not just in front of the TV. I mean having time together without a third party. Even if you do something together, like playing a game, it will allow you to have a private conversation, enjoy yourselves and have fun doing it.

Sometimes couples are together but still apart. They watch television together in silence, or one is watching his TV program upstairs, and the other watching their own program downstairs. Sometimes, if it is not watching TV, it is reading their books. I understand that there are times when couples will want to do their own separate things, but many times they hide behind wanting their own space just because things are not going right in the home. Instead of having a dialogue to deal with the situation, they say they need their space for a while. This can be devastating.

The pressures of work and the constant demands of raising children can easily and quickly draw couples apart. If the work load is shared, then one of the parties will not always be "too tired" at night. (You know what I mean.) How you share the workload during the day will determine how pleasant the night will be. How romantic you are with each other during the day will determine how ready for love the night will find you. How much you determine to resolve your differences quickly and restore relationship will determine how warm your bed will get.

TIME FOR SEX

Couples must make time for intimacy. Man is a sexual creature, and he has the need for periodic sex. Marriage is the right place for him to fulfill this need. The Scriptures declare:

> *But if they cannot contain, let them marry: for it is better to marry than to burn [with passion].*
> 1 Corinthians 7:9

> *Marriage is honourable in all, and the bed undefiled: but whoremongers and adulterers God will judge.*
> Hebrews 13:4

When you draw apart sexually or become casual about the need for sex, it is an indicator that you are growing apart in your relationship. Make time to be intimate and passionate with each other, and you will see its rewards in every area of married life.

ME TIME

Modern life can be so demanding that it seems as if everyone wants his or her own piece of you. This leaves you feeling drained, used and empty. You want your "Me Time." This is a time when you can be by yourself and do your own thing. You may spend time on your computer or playing a video game or going to the salon to do your hair, go window-shopping or do other girly stuff. Everyone needs his or her own "me time," and there must be time for it. After you have served your family well, it is not selfish to reward yourself with a few days of just doing what you want to do by yourself.

Have your me-time but, by all means, use it to recoup your strength to continue life. You need that. You may want to visit friends and family or just read a new book. Whatever you do, don't neglect your me-time.

It is also good that a time is set apart for the husband to have his me-time, if possible during the same time the wife is having hers.

TIME TO NURTURE

A plant need nurture in order to survive, a child needs love and nurture to survive and love and marriage need nurturing if they are to grow and become even more pleasant, like that rose you planted. A good-looking garden does not just appear. Someone has to take time to nurture it. In the very same way, a good marriage does not just appear. The two of you must work at it.

Working to have a good marriage is much like taking care of a baby or nurturing a garden. You have to work in that dirt, do some digging, fertilizing and watering. In the marriage, there is a lot of work (like changing all of those dirty diapers (nappies). Some people want

UNDERSTANDING HOW TO PROPERLY DIVIDE YOUR TIME

their marriage to bring itself to the level it should be without them having to expend any effort, but it doesn't work that way. Many give up far too quickly on their marriage, without working on it.

Couples need to take time occasionally to evaluate their marriage and their love for each other, to see if it is appreciating or depreciating. They need to weed out the things that are making the value of their home depreciated and add things that would increase the value of their home. It would be a good idea to make such a check every six months or so. At the very least, it should be done every year. Work at your marriage. The problem with your marriage is not the marriage itself; it's you.

Couples need to talk about how they can improve on their communication skills, their sex life and their money management, how to deal with third parties, like relatives and friends. Couples need to learn how to juggle the responsibilities of work and home and how to share the workload and to the management of the children. Many times, because these things are not communicated, life in the home becomes frustrating, and each party begins to lash out at the other, thinking that the other party is the problem. The problem is shared, just as everything else is shared.

The family calendar is completely full. It has God time, work time, playtime, nurture time and me time, and all of these things eat at and make their demands of you. They are all very important and should not be neglected. I believe if we make time for all of these, life will become less stressful and demanding, and your home will become balanced, having all the T's crossed and I's dotted. Both parties need to work at making their home pleasant for all. This is very important because God wants our marriage to be a *Marriage made in Heaven.*

CHAPTER 9

Understanding Blessings that Can Destroy

Blessings that God intended to bless a marriage with can be turned into curses that will destroy it. Here are a few to watch out for.

CAREER

Man was created in the image and likeness of God and was created to be the provider for the family. In this twenty-first century, we know that both man and wife often work to provide for the needs of the home, but the fact still remains that the husband is the designated provider.

With the wife, however, there must be a balance. It is my take that if the husband takes his place as provider of the family, the wife should not spend so much time working that she neglects her duties as homemaker. I understand that husband and wife can come to an agreement about how they want things to happen in their own home, but if there is no such agreement and the woman decides to pursue making money and neglects her duty in the home, this can cause serious conflicts.

Marriage is a compromise and no two homes are the same. The Scriptures tell us:

Therefore as the church is subject unto Christ, so let the wives be to their own husbands in every thing.
Ephesians 5:24

Therefore what the husband allows in this circumstance stands. If he can provide adequately for his home, the wife can limit her time at work. If the wife has a more lucrative and demanding work they both want her to keep, and they both decide that the husband should limit his own time at work, that is their decision. The problem arises when both work so much that they have no time for each other and for the children. For the sake of the future of a marriage, conflicts must be avoided at all costs. When a husband insists that he play his own role and the woman play hers, both must comply. This is the will of God.

These days, women are sometimes in more lucrative positions than their husbands and therefore earn more than them. Some men have a problem with their wife being a "career women," especially if this prevents her from fulfilling her rightful role as wife and mother.

I may sound old-fashioned, but I believe in a "career man" and a "woman with a career," not a "career woman." If the man is the provider of the home, he should pursue a career that will pay him enough to bless his home. The woman, who serves in the capacity as "help" to her husband, may pursue a career, but she is woman, wife and mother first. If career comes first to both of them, such marriages will begin to experience conflicts. Husbands and wives need to understand their roles in the home and function within those roles.

LEARNING TO WORK TOGETHER

Many of the marriages between Hollywood actors don't last long because they are both career people. The Hollywood marriages that seemed to last are those in which one of them pursues a career and the other is the homemaker. Many marriages between Christian ministers also fail because the woman has her own ministry, independent of her husband's ministry. I firmly believe that a man and his wife, if they are both ministers, should work together under the same ministry—even if their ministries are different. They can have two or more arms of their ministry, as many arms as they would like, but when they work together, they are able to be together and work around the same people. It is my opinion that, in this way, they can better manage their work schedule by working together rather than apart from each other.

Business couples can work better together as a family business than in distinct individual businesses. Being together, working together, and making money together can help strengthen couples, help them protect each other and become more transparent with each other. The two have become one, so let them work as one.

It is rather unfortunate that many married people still live as individuals rather than as couples. Many, although married, still seek individual dreams, rather than a collective one. They compete as to who can have the greater income, rather than working together toward a communal income. No wonder some become greedy, seek a divorce, and try to skin the other for all they can get. Many divorces expose the truth of how couples have been operating as individuals during their time as a married couple.

The bottom line is this: The wife should be a suitable helper for her husband, a suitable helpmeet for him. She should not forget that. Women, you are not the provider of the home; your husband is; and what you are to do is to help him, not to compete with him or to show that you are equally or even more capable than he. Because you are married, you are now a team.

MONEY

Money, power and fame should all be blessings that enrich the family, but often they do the opposite, breaking the family apart. With some men, for example, the more money they have, the more girlfriends they seem to accumulate. The more power they have, the worse they treat their spouse.

For some, their gadgets now have all their love, instead of their spouse. Their car becomes their babe (or their clothes, shoes, or house, etc). Some men even give their partners orders not to touch certain things in their home. Others, when they become successful, no longer consider their partner of the same class. They have become "too good" for them.

With some, their partners are only good for them during their times of struggle, not in their moments of success. They soon forget that their partner was supporting them and making sacrifices for them to achieve their goals. After the goals have been achieved, the partner is no longer needed.

UNDERSTANDING BLESSINGS THAT CAN DESTROY

"OURS," NOT "MINE"

To help eradicate the individualistic culture rampant in marriages today, the first words that need to be changed are *I* and *me*. For those who are married the words *I* and *me* must be replaced with *we* and *our*. Couples must learn to save together and spend together. Save together for a house and then buy it together. Save together for a car, furniture, and a TV and then buy them together. Everything in the house should be *ours*, not *mine* or *yours*.

One couple quarreled so heatedly that they threatened to destroy each other's possessions. She wanted to destroy *his* television, and he wanted to destroy *her* washing machine. How foolish. A solid marriage must have a joint bank account from which they buy everything together. They must have regular house meetings in which they agree on their budget for the month, year, etc. Together they should develop a scale of preferences for spending, and then stick with it. The two must build together.

CHILDREN

> *Lo, children are an heritage of the* Lord *: and the fruit of the womb is his reward. As arrows are in the hand of a mighty man; so are children of the youth. Happy is the man that hath his quiver full of them: they shall not be ashamed, but they shall speak with the enemies in the gate.*
> Psalm 127:3-5

Children are, no doubt, a blessing from God, but they can also become a curse that destroys the marriage. Children born within the marriage, children born in another marriage or children born outside of marriage can all be a negative influence on your marriage. You, however, can prevent this from happening. Develop a plan as to how to maintain everyone united, how to train them and how to apply discipline when needed. If there is a disagreement in these areas, or if nothing has been laid down, it inevitably leads to conflict in the marriage.

THE ROLE OF CHILDREN IN THE HOME

- Children must obey their parents in the Lord (see Ephesians 6:1 and Colossians 3:20).
- Children must honor their parents (see Exodus 20:12 and Ephesians 6:2).
- Fathers must not provoke their children to wrath (see Ephesians 6:4 and Colossians 3:21).

Often there are conflicts when children are born in another marriage or with another outside the marital home. Abraham had to send Ishmael and his mum away, and he give gifts to Keturah's children and sent them away too, to avoid conflicts (see Genesis 21:14 and 25:6). Jephthah's brothers kicked him out of their father's house because he was born of a prostitute (see Judges 11:1-3). There can still be conflicts in homes where children are born of the same parents, as in the case of Cain and Abel and Jacob and Esau. There were conflicts when one was preferred over the other. Parents must make sure that their children are in control, love one another and remain in subjection to their parents.

The husband and his wife must make sure they agree on how to raise their children together. They must also make sure they do not disagree in front of their children or condemn each other in front of them. Children have a way of setting their parents against each other. Parents must be aware of this and refuse to fall into this trap.

In the early years of our marriage, our children would ask me, for example, for an ice cream. If I refused their request, they would go behind my back and ask their mum for the ice cream. Mary, not knowing that they had already asked me and I had said no, might sometimes tell them to go and get it. They would get the ice cream and then pass by me so that I could see it and would say, "Mum said I could have it."

We settled that problem quickly. When any of the children asked us for something or whether they could go out, for instance, the first question either of us would ask is, "Have you asked your mum?" or "have you asked your dad?" If the answer was yes, the next question was, "What did he [or she] say?" If the answer was no, then it was "no." One of the children commented on this new strategy, "You two agree on everything." That was exactly the message we wanted to send.

SEEKING HELP

Husbands and wives often need help. Both should look to someone they admire and want to emulate and agree to make them a mentor. It is best to begin this in courtship.

Usually a mentor should be someone apart from relatives. Although relatives can help, this should be someone who will be there to guide and help you in your courtship and then in your marriage. Whatever you do, do not take your courtship or marriage problems to an inexperienced friend. Some might even envy your relationship and give you wrong advice that will cause you to lose each other. Seek out more experienced people with whom you can talk about your courtship or marraiage. Your pastors are always there to give you spiritual and prayerful guidance. Some churches may designate some experienced couple to guide you through your courtship and marriage.

It is also good to attend marriage seminars. There helpful tips will be provided that could help your marriage. You do not need to receive every single point others have passed on, but take onboard what the two of you can agree on that is beneficial to your courtship or mariage.

It is important that the two of you agree that if there comes a time in your relationship when either of you feels you can no longer handle a given situation, without the consent of the other, you will confide in your mentors and seek their help. This is important because it may be the thing that could save your marriage in the future. Go for the type of marriage God intended yours to be, a *Marriage Made in Heaven*.

CHAPTER 10

Understanding the Importance of Good Communication

I CAN'T HEAR YOU

I have come to the conclusion, through two decades of marriage, that men and women don't speak the same language, so to speak. A woman's language changes, depending on the mood she is in. Sometimes you can't take her literally. You have to hear her with your heart, not with your mind, so to speak. To a common man, what the woman is saying doesn't make sense. You need to understand her language.

Men usually speak straight, but our problem is that often we don't hear what is being said by our wives. I don't mean this literally, of course. Either we don't understand the language being used, or we are preoccupied with what other guys have said about this subject, guys who themselves have no clue and are equally confused about how women speak. I have tried teaching women to speak men's language, but they simply can't do it. I have now come to the conclusion that it is up to men to understand how their women speak. If we can't communicate on the level of our wives, there will always be miscommunication in our homes and this will result in chaos.

We must learn (1) How communication works, and (2) How our individual partner speaks. Our eye contact and body gestures, tone of voice, touch, apparent attitude or reaction after an incidence, and crying or laughing are all part of the way we speak. Communication can be verbal or non-verbal.

Men and women speak, even when they are not speaking. In general terms, women speak more than men, but there are some women who don't speak a lot and some men who speak a lot. Always communicate, whatever the cost. Avoid the silent treatment, retaliation and withholding sexual relationship from your partner. Talk over everything and try to arrive at a peaceful compromise. This is healthy for your relationship.

One of the areas men and women have problems with is saying, "I love you." Men, many times, not know why they need to say "I love you" every day. They believe that "I love you" should be seen in what they do, not necessarily in words. They believe their love should be seen in their integrity, values and the things they do to please their spouse. To a woman, however, a verbal assurance of love brings her a feeling of appreciation and security. She needs that. Recognize that we speak on different wavelengths, and give your woman what she needs.

How unfortunate that Players know better than many husbands how to communicate with women. They specialize in speaking a woman's language. Do you sometimes wonder why a woman falls for the wrong guy? This is the reason. They know how to appeal to women.

UNDERSTANDING THE IMPORTANCE OF GOOD COMMUNICATION

"Do I *have* to communicate with my wife in that way?" some may ask. Well, if it means keeping the woman you love happy why wouldn't you want to do it. You may be asking the wrong question. Developing good communication skills and talking with your spouse about everything in a civilized manner helps build understanding and friendship in the marriage. Here are some tips that can be helpful:

- Never go to sleep at night and leave a contentious situation pending.
- Develop good listening skills.
- Never assume. Always ask why?
- Give each other turns to talk, have a listening ear, and try to understand what is been said.
- Pull together, not apart. Stop trying to score points.
- Always compliment your spouse and let any criticism be constructive in nature.
- Never forget to say, "I'm sorry" when you have messed up.
- Never stop saying, "I love you."

BUILDING COMMUNICATION

And the man and his wife were both naked and were not embarrassed or ashamed in each other's presence.
Genesis 2:25

Good communication must be built on the following:

Truth: *It is good to talk about your lives, your pasts and your hopes for the future. Do not try to build on lies. Do* *not be embarrassed about the truth. The other party must know whom they are wanting to marry. We all have good and bad qualities, and we all have some kind of past. It is good the other party knows now rather than later. If the other party comes to discover something about you through other means, you might appear to be a liar and the other party may well begin to have doubts about you and to wonder if there are not other things you are hiding from them. Do not compromise the truth. If the other party cannot handle the truth about you and your past now, he or she may not be able to handle it after you are married. Don't save it until you get married.*

Honesty: *Be honest. Let you partner know they can count on you to tell them the truth. You must be honest at all times, regardless of the consequences.*

Dependability: *Your partner must count on you to do what you have said you would do. Never say one thing and do another. You must be dependable. Someone said, "If you say you can do it, that is confidence, but doing it is competence." Don't just show confidence; prove competence.*

Trust: *The two of you will become vulnerable before each other and you must be true to each other. Do not, at any time, use the other's weaknesses against him or her. You must give each other the assurance of belonging to each other, regardless of your past and/or present problems. It is upon such assurance that openness can develop. Do*

UNDERSTANDING THE IMPORTANCE OF GOOD COMMUNICATION

not break your promises to each other, and do not turn against those things you have already built on.

WHEN ONE PARTY BECOMES UNCOOPERATIVE

The place no one wants to come to in marriage is when one party becomes uncooperative and unresponsive. What can the other party do? If both of them are looking for help, counseling and other things can be done to amend things. But what happens if one of the parties involved doesn't want to have anything to do with any of that? We all need to understand that there will come a time in our lives, whether in marriage or not, that we need to let God have His way in our lives and in that of our loved ones. The only things we can do in cases where one party no longer is responsive is:

- Continue loving that person.
- Continue praying for that person.

Sometimes we need to go further, by fasting and engaging in spiritual warfare in an attempt to save our marriage. Time also has a way of bringing healing and deliverance. So make room for time, and let God do His work. Do whatever it takes to have a *Marriage Made in Heaven*.

Chapter 11

Understanding the Promise: "Till Death Us Do Part"

HONORING YOUR VOWS

When you got married, you made a vow saying: "Till death us do part." That vow should be honored at all times, and it can only be annulled if one marriage partner commits adultery:

> *But I say unto you, That whosoever shall put away his wife, saving for the cause of fornication, causeth her to commit adultery: and whosoever shall marry her that is divorced committeth adultery.*   Matthew 5:32

If both parties were unsaved at the time of the marriage and then one of them receives the Lord Jesus as their Savior and Lord, sometimes the other party won't want to remain in the marriage anymore. In this case, the saved party can be released from the marriage:

> *And the woman which hath an husband that believeth not, and if he be pleased to dwell with her, let her not leave*

UNDERSTANDING THE PROMISE: "TILL DEATH US DO PART"

him. For the unbelieving husband is sanctified by the wife, and the unbelieving wife is sanctified by the husband :else were your children unclean; but now are they holy. But if the unbelieving depart, let him depart. A brother or a sister is not under bondage in such cases: but God hath called us to peace.   1 Corinthians 7:13-15

We need to understand, however, that we are not *compelled* to leave our wives or husbands if they commit adultery. Our Lord has made room for forgiveness and reconciliation. We also should not get rid of our unsaved spouses if they still want to live with us. If, however, someone does not want to live with you because of your faith, you cannot deny your faith in order to keep them.

Today believers divorce for any reason at all. I am not aware of any other reasons the Bible gives for divorce. I do believe that you can separate from each other for a time in circumstances where the relationship has become violent, abusive or life-threatening, while you are seeking help. Help can be sought for both the offending and the offended parties during this separation period, and then, hopefully, you can get back together. Other than these, the Bible does not give any other reason for divorce.

WHAT IF I HAVE BROKEN MY VOWS?

I want to speak now to those who have been divorced. Your divorce may have come as a result of marital infidelity, the unsaved departing, violence in the home, a partner absconding from the home, or a partner becoming ill or impotent. Your vow, "Till death us do part," may have already been broken as a result of any of these situations. Your question is: What do I do now?

I believe the first step would be to make an attempt to seek reconciliation and the restoration of your marriage. If this is no longer possible because of the complexity of the situation (for example, the other party has already re-married), then you have a decision to make. If the divorce came as a result of marital unfaithfulness, then it is my personal belief that you are free to remarry. The same is true in the case that an unbelieving party decides to leave a believer:

> *But if the unbelieving depart, let him depart. A brother or a sister is not under bondage in such cases: but God hath called us to peace.*   1 Corinthians 7:15

What does it mean when it says *"a brother or sister is not under bondage in such cases"*? It means that he or she is no longer bound to the marriage under these circumstances. For those who are still married, honor your vows.

HONOR YOUR MARRIAGE BED

> *Marriage is honourable in all, and the bed undefiled: but whoremongers and adulterers God will judge.*
>   Hebrews 13:4

You show your spouse honor by respecting your marriage bed, and you respect your marriage bed by not sharing it with any third party. In Christian marriage, no kissing, petting, caressing, or inappropriate touching is allowed with a third party. That would show disrespect to your spouse and be a grave dishonor. And it might very well destroy the marriage. God made very severe penalties against it. He said: *"Adulterers God will judge!"*

RECONCILIATION AND RESTORATION

In countless cases of divorce in the past, God has been faithful to restore couples and to reconcile them to resume their marital union in happiness, and He is still doing it today. Jesus is the same yesterday, today and forever, and because He hates divorce, He is always pleased to see the reconciliation and reuniting of married couples. If you are divorced, dare to believe God to help you too. Then, take a step of faith in that direction, and see what He will do.

Seek help from qualified spiritual leaders through counselling and prayer, but you must be the one to make up your mind to do whatever is necessary to restore your marriage. God will do the rest. Always remember:

For with God nothing shall be impossible. Luke 1:37

GOD HATES DIVORCE

God wants us to honor our vows. He is a covenant keeper, and He requires the same from us. Marriage was His first ordinance, and He has said that what He has joined no one should separate.

The Scriptures also warn us against dealing treacherously with our wife. God says He hates it:

*Yet ye say, Wherefore? Because the L*ORD *hath been witness between thee and the wife of thy youth, against whom* *thou hast dealt treacherously: yet is she thy companion, and the wife of thy covenant. And did not he make one? Yet had he the residue of the spirit. And wherefore one? That he might seek a godly seed. Therefore take heed to your spirit, and let none deal treacherously against the wife of his youth. For the* LORD *, the God of Israel, saith that he hateth putting away.* Malachi 2:14-16

Don't be guilty of doing what God hates. Instead, do what God loves, and you will have a *Marriage Made in Heaven*.

The Conclusion

I do not, in any way, profess to be a marriage guru or authority on this subject. My purpose here has been to share with others what the Lord has taught me and also my own personal experiences in this regard. I am still learning and also still going through the challenges we all go through in marriage. Jesus told us that we can know the truth and the truth will set us free. I believe that these truths recorded here will set your marriage free.

My wish for us all is that we have a happy marriage, and I believe that our Lord will see us all through, as we demonstrate His love to each other and seek to keep the sacred union He initiated.

This book would not have a full conclusion if I did not add that not everyone is called into the marriage union. Some people are called to be celibates. Don't force them to marry, and please respect their call. Some are born celibates, and some have made themselves celibates for the work of Christ. A celibate will make a disaster of marriage if you force them to marry.

> *But he said unto them, All men cannot receive this saying, save they to whom it is given. For there are some eunuchs, which were so born from their mother's womb:*

and there are some eunuchs, which were made eunuchs of men: and there be eunuchs, which have made themselves eunuchs for the kingdom of heaven's sake. He that is able to receive it, let him receive it.   Matthew 19:11-12

There are others who, after a divorce (for whatever reason) or after the death of their loved ones, choose to live a celibate life. Please feel free to do so. Your love for Jesus surpasses love for a man or for a woman. Enjoy your celibate life to the full and be faithful to you Lord and Savior Jesus Christ.

Besides, we are all married to Him and, as His Bride, let's be faithful to Him. He is coming soon to take us to be with Him, and we shall reign with Him forever and ever.

Now may the grace of our LORD *and Savior Jesus Christ, the love of God and the fellowship of the Holy Spirit, rest, remain and abide with us and our loved ones now and forever more. Amen!*

Always remember:

Now, have a *Marriage Made In Heaven*

Other Books by Desmond Thomas

Desmond Thomas

Be Delivered and stay Delivered

The Believer's Handbook to Deliverance from the Power of Darkness

Desmond Thomas

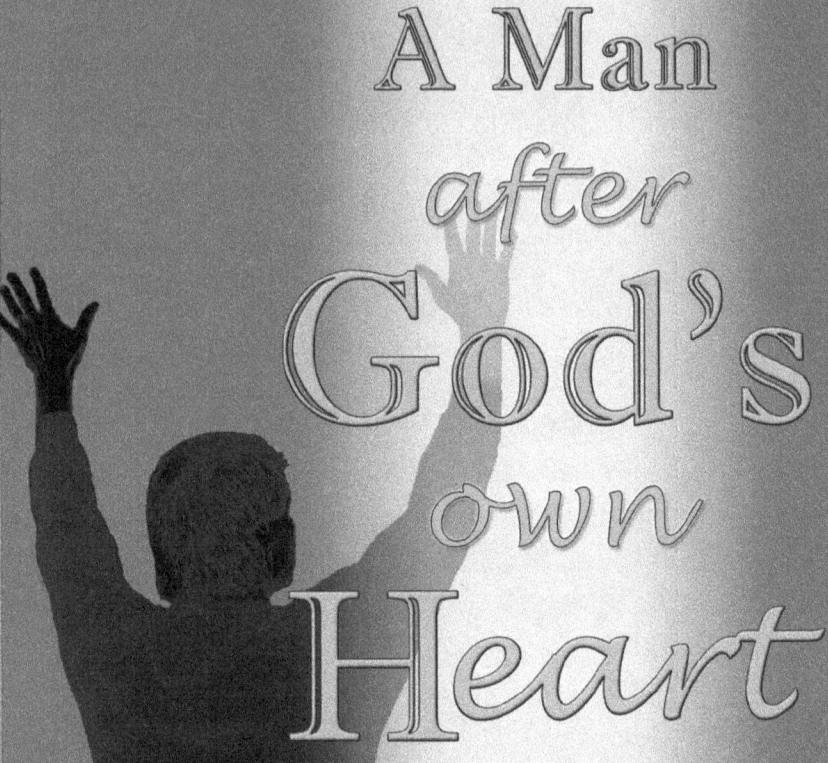

A Man after God's own Heart

Moving Successfully Toward Spiritual Continuity, Establishment and Leadership

Desmond Alphonso Thom

Desmond Thomas

BE HEALED AND STAY HEALED

The Beliver's Handbook on How to Be Healed, Stay Healed and Administer Healing to Others

Author Contact Page

Those wishing to correspond with the author may do so at the following addresses:

In Africa:
Pastor Desmond A. Thomas
Ministry of the Word
P.M.B. 365
Freetown, Sierra Leone
West Africa

In Europe:
Ministry of the Word
desmondthomasministries@yahoo.com
www.facebook.com/desmondthomasministries

In the U.S.:
Ministry of the Word
c/o McDougal & Associates
www.thepublishedword.com

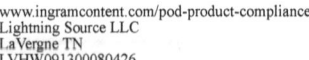
www.ingramcontent.com/pod-product-compliance
Lightning Source LLC
LaVergne TN
LVHW091300080426
835510LV00007B/343